Though born into wealth, Vera was plunged i
recent history. By the grace of God, she survive
Rouge's killing fields brings perspective to a
plight of those under communist rule, and insp ... atter what.

—Lisa Worthey Smith, award-winning author

There is no greater testimony of faith than real-life experiences. Vera's experiences are more horrific than anyone I have ever met and yet God has used all Vera's good, bad, and ugly life experiences to form her into the Christian she is today. She shares her story as a gift of encouragement to each of us and to her grandchildren and future generations to encourage us to never give up, to hold on to hope, and to always turn to God for help.

—Sue Copeland, St. Francis of Assisi, Chapin,
Spiritual Growth and Discipleship Liaison

I read this book in about three days. It follows the life of the author, Vera Crenshaw, and her family through years of pain, suffering, and loss set in Cambodia during the tumultuous time of Pol Pot's terroristic reign. It was a very good depiction of the stark reality of the cruel Khmer Rouge government and the inhumanities of man inflicted on his fellow man. I understand why such a long recovery time is needed after an extended traumatic encounter such as this. I liked this book and was fascinated to understand the "killing fields" of Cambodia. It is the story of how Vera overcame tremendous hardships through her steadfast relationship with God.

—Barbara McKellar

When Pam and I read the full realm of adversity (self-doubt, physical injury/illness, rejection, poverty, losing a loved one, and struggling to succeed) that Vera and her family experienced, I saw the reality of "If God is for us, who can be against us?" (Romans 8:31). Vera's continued faith in God and eventual acknowledgment of Jesus's saving grace is a strong testimony of why we need to embrace God and Jesus in our lives today.

—Rene and Pamela Harrell, retired ship repair
project manager / design consultant

Until the Day Dawns—what a story of grit, strength, survival. Vera is such a beautiful, loving person. I am lucky enough to call her a friend, and this experience she has so bravely chosen to share with us shows how she is this beautiful friend and human being today. Thank you for sharing this experience with us and thank you for being such a positive force in this world.

—Matthew J. Zachariah

Vera Crenshaw lived through one of the most horrific examples of human cruelty that we have seen in recorded history: the killing fields of Cambodia. In *Until the Day Dawns*, the reader experiences her visceral reactions to that cruelty. On the other side is a woman who, despite her loss, has experienced life, love, and faith. This book is a story of resilience that benefits any reader.

—The Reverend Doug Graul, Vicar at St. Francis of Assisi Episcopal Church

From a life of wealth and family love to a long path through the valley of death, from the promise generated by the finest education to years spent trying to fathom the realities of a new country, supporting her children in any way available and enduring marital strife, Vera has turned again and again to God as a source of strength and unwavering love. Now she shares those experiences in order to testify to her faith and her ever increasing devotion to sharing that strength with others. An amazing story and an engrossing read!

—Pamela Lichty

This is an uplifting story of the strength of an individual who, no matter how difficult the circumstances, continued to persevere to survive and not to lose her basic human dignity. Vera Crenshaw lived through one of the most oppressive and cruel regimes in the world's history. Through her desire for life combined with her intelligence, she miraculously lived through the regime of the communist dictator Pol Pot. Her story includes a tale of courage against the horrors and brutality that he brought to Cambodia. While constantly facing death and starvation, Vera exemplified the dignity of the human spirit. It's a story of survival and transformation. It is ultimately more savage and horrible than one can imagine. Vera's story is both a testament of her own inner strength and character and an acknowledgment of the peace that only God can bring to everyone.

—Taeko "Terri" Kerr

Until the Day Dawns by Vera Crenshaw is a powerful reminder that God is at work in the holiest places of our world and lives. This compelling, true narrative will take you into a world of privilege, then danger, oppression, and suffering, then lead you unerringly to a place of resilience and peace founded in an unshakeable faith in the Lord Jesus Christ. Vera Crenshaw writes with a clear and direct force that draws the reader into a world few in the West have experienced or can even imagine. This is a book that reads like an action novel yet with the gentleness and compassion of one who has experienced life's tragedies and triumphs firsthand.

—Terry Burnett, CLE director, South Carolina Bar

This book is a journey through the life of Vera. It touches on the love of her family and how this love and the things she learned through her parents affected everything she did in her life. Most of the struggles are unbelievable, and her endurance and will to go on is inspirational. You know, God was with her the whole time, especially when she was supposed to be kill three times. Yet she survived. Although many obstacles, disappointments, tragedies, and a horrible mother-in-law were constantly bombarding her, Vera's faith and love of family kept her going. It is my pleasure to endorse this book.

—Cathy Schwalm

Until the Day DAWNS

A True Story of Faith, Hope, and Perseverance

VERA CRENSHAW

BROOKSTONE PUBLISHING GROUP

Birmingham, Alabama

Until the Day Dawns

Brookstone Publishing Group
An imprint of Iron Stream Media
100 Missionary Ridge
Birmingham, AL 35242
IronStreamMedia.com

Library of Congress Control Number: 2023907275

Cover design by twolineSTUDIO.com

ISBN: 978-1-949856-98-9 (paperback)
ISBN: 978-1-949856-99-6 (eBook)

1 2 3 4 5—27 26 25 24 23

You will do well to pay attention as to a lamp shining in a dark place, until the day dawns and the morning star rises in your hearts.

—2 Peter 1:19 ESV

IN LOVING MEMORY

This memoir seeks to honor the memory of my parents, Kuy Peou and Mam Sa Man.

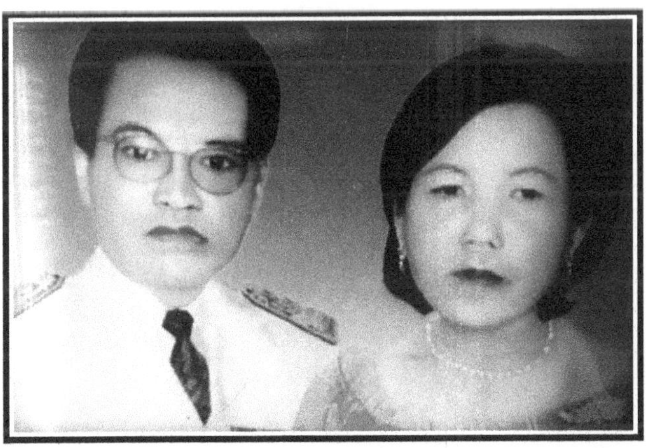

This memoir also is written to honor the memory of my son's father, Chin Seng Heang.

Special honor to my loving brothers, Peou Visothara and Peou Metrey. Their memories have inspired me to live when I did not know if I would survive.

Extended dedication to adopted brother Peou Nem, uncles Som Kim San and Som Kim Sonn, and my many relatives along with all those who suffered and died under the Khmer Rouge regime.

I miss you all so very much.

TABLE OF CONTENTS

PREFACE

My luxurious life ended when the Khmer Rouge regime took power in my home country of Cambodia.

Everyone has his or her battles. It's a gross injustice to compare one's difficulties with that of another. However, you might agree that war requires extreme endurance for sheer survival. For years, I witnessed and endured brutalities most will never encounter in the "killing fields" you've probably heard about. I came out alive, but the horrifying memories are embedded within me and continue to shape my life.

Decades later, I have gone through drastic changes to get to where I am today. Through ongoing trials and tribulations, and with God's help, I have survived loss and intense hardships. I have learned that life is a true testimony of perseverance, but God gives us victory!

With Him, I will survive!
Vera Peou Crenshaw

MY FAMILY AND ADOPTED FAMILY

My Parents

My father, Mr. Kuy Peou, a judge, senator, diplomat, minister of religion, and the CEO of a royal newspaper. My mother, Mam Sa Man (dearly known as Som Kim Sath), an entrepreneur. She owned gem mines, rubber tree plantations, rice fields, and rental properties, and she raised nine children.

Their Children	Nickname	English Name
Peou Visothara (son)	Boung Ra	Scott
Peou Metrey (son)	Bross Tom	
Peou Kuna (daughter)	Srey Na	Vera
Peou Sithik (son)	Bross Ran	Frederick
Peou Mohatheary (son)	Bross Notch	
Peou Phallabobrick (son)	Bross Match	Rick
Peou Yuvida (daughter)	Srey Da	
Peou Dararong (son)	Bross Nong	David
Peou Charnay (daughter)	Srey Nay	

Plus Their Three Adopted Children

Peou Nem
Peou Noy
Peou Nith

Chapter 1

LIFE BEFORE THE WAR

The early 1970s
Cambodia

The chauffeur opened the rear passenger door and half-bowed toward me while I climbed in and sat. He secured the door and then stood, smoothing his spotless white uniform. Inside the clean air-conditioned vehicle, I nodded toward him, indicating I was safely in my seat and approved of his appearance. With that permission, he slid into the driver's seat and adjusted his white cap. My parents expected nothing less than perfection, and so did I.

I discreetly checked for any stray morsels of breakfast that might have remained on my face. The local bakery delivered fresh-baked French bread every morning. I had dipped mine in sweetened condensed milk. Decadent but fabulous.

Satisfied my face didn't carry any crumbs, I admired the beauty of the bustling vibrant capital city, Phnom Penh. We'd moved here when I was seven or eight years old, after my father had been elected to the Senate. Up until then, we lived in the province of Kampong Cham, where my father worked at the Tribunal Justice as a judge.

He now reported to a new office in the Ministry of the National Assembly, a three-story building with a golden spire on top. Though quite ornate, that building paled in comparison to the royal palace. Every time I rode through the city, I searched for a glimpse of the palace. Its multiple golden peaks glimmered in the morning sun, reminding us of the high standing of the royal family.

I gazed out the window at the busy people on the streets. So many barely made a living. Others found work in the garment industry or became nurses or truck drivers and lived in middle-class areas of town.

We continued toward the university, where I studied. The fragrant aroma of the rumduol blossoms growing in the parks filtered into the interior of the car. I half-closed my eyes as my lungs filled with the enticing smell, holding in the sweet scent as long as I could before I exhaled. I'd often heard men comparing the beauty of a woman to these lovely flowers.

Perhaps one day I would wear a rumduol ear cuff at my royal wedding. I met the king's son, Crown Prince Norodom Naradipo when I attended a royal event with my father. We became friends and now were spoken of as a couple. We saw each other occasionally and corresponded regularly. I shifted my sunglasses and surveyed the capital city, imagining the glamour and opulence of life by his side.

Of course, my parents had already arranged a customary Khmer wedding to the son of their best friend. (*Khmer* being the ancient word for *Cambodian.*) He was still away at school in France, finishing his doctoral studies.

But, before that, as the eldest daughter, I needed to finish my education and learn all I could about my parents' businesses.

A whippoorwill distracted me as he swooped past us in pursuit of an insect. I often saw these aerobatic birds around my parents' rice fields snatching the rice moths and other insects in flight.

The rice fields were a good income source, but my soul thrived at our rubber tree plantation. All nine of us siblings worked together on the massive plantation. Knowing the rich Cambodian soil and climate were both perfect for growing robust rubber trees, my mother had used her inheritance to purchase over a million young rubber tree plants. She had them planted in neat rows across thousands of acres of land. We employed several full-time workers to manage the vast property.

I allowed the lull of the car to transport my mind to the beautiful plantation and imagined sitting in the shade, inhaling the cool fresh air. The horses would be grazing in the sun. Chickens and geese would be clucking while they raised their babies or sat on fresh eggs. Before the rainy season began, the groundskeepers would be gathering fruit for the merchants who came weekly to purchase produce.

People would be pumping water where my father had installed a manual hand-pump well at the corner of the street.

Nearly twenty-four hours a day someone pumped clean water for their homes and families on our plantation.

My parents had spent a great deal of time with their employees preparing our land and clearing it of any debris, dry weeds, and grass. They also built cottages of hardwood and bamboo on the land, and we spent many weekends there. We had a life of luxury in the city, but our weekends on the plantation, at the beach, or in the mountains, were treasured family times for me.

Each year that passed, the rubber trees branched out and transformed the area into even more of a verdant green paradise. Within the next couple of years, the trees would produce enough rubber sap for a good harvest and continue producing this liquid gold for many years to come.

My mother told us that once the trees produced enough sap, it would generate enough money that they would be able to send all of us to be educated in Europe, the US, or anywhere else we wanted to go.

I smiled. Traveling to expand my education sounded like a fun option. We had already studied English and French at private schools. Now eighteen, I still had time to see the world before marrying and taking over part of the family business.

I learned as much as I could about some of my parents' other businesses. After all, even if I didn't marry the prince, I wanted to honor my precious parents by becoming an astute businesswoman and a suitable wife for my future husband. I did everything I could to prepare myself for a life of social standing and comfort with cooks and maids and everything I could ever want.

The car slowed to a stop and I roused from my daydream. While the driver opened the door and waited for me to get out, I gathered my things for class and allowed a demure smile to form from the idea of my current life and family and the wonderful possibilities awaiting me. I stepped out of the air-conditioned car into the warm breeze and heard the door close behind me.

I felt a twinge of sympathy for the young lady about my age who bicycled past me. Dressed in a cotton sarong, she probably lived in a tiny bamboo home with parents who farmed. None of them would ever own the modern clothes or be acquainted with the lifestyle our family enjoyed. With my father a high-ranking politician and multiple high-income family businesses, thankfully, I would never truly understand her level of poverty.

Striding with confidence toward my class, I directed my thoughts to the important things of the day. Will I receive another letter from the prince today? Will this one claim my heart and my adult life? Will my arranged fiancé come home from France to start a life with me? Will our family spend the weekend at the beach, the mountains, or the plantation?

Life was good and I had no intention of ever settling for anything less.

Chapter 2

CHANGE IS COMING

When I came home from college that day, I stopped in the carport to visit the family mynah bird.

"Hello. Hello," he squawked.

"Hello." I peered into his cage. "Have you been a good bird today?"

With his sleek black wings out slightly, he hopped from one perch to another and settled in a pose highlighting his handsome profile. He opened his flame-colored beak and answered, "Good bird. Good bird."

I opened my hands to show him I didn't bring him any food this time. "Sorry, maybe next time."

"Next time. Vroom, vroom."

This guy always threw in engine noises when he wanted attention. People often rewarded him with a snack after an engine performance.

An unsuspecting fly zipped into his cage. He snatched it and managed to gurgle "Good bird," while he stretched out his neck to swallow. "Hello. Hello."

I smiled at my vocal feathered friend. He more than earned his luxurious lifestyle by keeping the insect population down, not to mention the entertainment he provided. "Yes. You are a good bird."

"Good bird. Vroom vroom."

When I walked inside, the fragrance of roses arranged in a vase on a table greeted me, but my thoughts focused on whether my maid remembered the instructions I gave her that morning.

When I came into the house, a maid immediately asked me to go see my mother.

"Is she sick?"

"No. But she wants to see you right away. She's on the balcony in their room."

I hurried to the third floor and found my mother, Mom, on the sky balcony. "Mom? You wanted to see me?"

"Come in." She turned to face me, laid down the papers she held, and motioned for me to sit. She clasped her hands in front of her. "You know the husband we had arranged for you to marry is still at school in France."

"Yes. I've known that since I was fifteen."

She looked out toward the city. "I'm sure you've heard of some of the political unrest."

"Yes." I wiped my palms on my pants. This conversation had a heaviness I didn't expect.

She looked at me and sighed with a mix of compassion and concern. "Well, your father and I believe it would be in your best interest to marry someone else now, rather than wait any longer for him to return."

My heart leaped to my throat. Has the prince asked for my hand?

"You know of Chin Seng Heang."

I exhaled my hopeful breath and thought for a moment. "The governor?" He's at least a decade older than I am.

"Yes. He is quite wealthy and will be able to provide for you in case . . ." She looked around the room for a few seconds before she focused on me and raised her eyebrows with resolve. "It is settled and you two will be married in a few months. That way . . ." She covered her face with both hands and wept.

"What's wrong, Mom? Why can't I wait?"

She dabbed her eyes with a linen handkerchief she pulled from her waistband. "I don't want you to worry, but you do need to be informed. Since Lon Nol has been elected, disturbing rumors are going around. Our king has already aligned himself with communists, and we just don't know what might be about to happen. You need to have the protection and security Heang can offer."

While she sobbed and patted her face, I recalled that my parents had spoken of communism and the plight of Vietnam, the country to our east and south. My history lessons raced through my head. Communism had spread from China to North Vietnam and gained control. South Vietnam still resisted, trying to retain their freedom.

In years past, King Sihanouk had publicly asserted his neutrality and stayed away from the Vietnam conflict. He argued to the French that Cambodia, Khmer, could fall into communist hands as Vietnam had. Using the French term for "red," *rouge*—a nod to the color of the Chinese flag—he warned of a Khmer Rouge, if we remained under French colonization.

With communist control threatening to overtake South Vietnam, the king accepted aid from the US. However, when the US tried to convince him to come under the protection of the Southeast Asia Treaty Organization, his public speeches sounded as if he feared the US might be trying to shift Cambodia to a democratic government, meaning he might lose power.

Then he accepted millions in economic aid from the Chinese, fueling suspicions that Sihanouk had softened to communist ideas. Some of my friends told me they heard rumors of some of the democratic leaders questioning whether they should continue their loyalty to a monarchy with communist leanings.

Even though he had publicly opposed the communist agenda, Sihanouk agreed to allow the communists to transport Chinese communist military equipment from North Vietnam to the battlefronts in South Vietnam by way of a trail through Cambodia near the Vietnamese border.

Every deal he made with the Chinese added to the corruption. The US had already severed ties with Cambodia and bombed the trail, trying to give the South Vietnamese a chance to defend themselves. Meanwhile, China, Czechoslovakia, and the Soviet Union increased their military aid to us in Cambodia, obviously their allies now.

Did she suspect we were about to go to war?

"Of course, I'll do whatever you and Pa think is best." I refused to let my throat choke on the words. I would always honor my parents, but this fast change in my marriage plans and Mom's tears told me they were acting in desperation and my dreams were about to fall apart.

My mother blinked to clear out the remaining tears and said, "He will come this week. You two can get to know each other before the wedding."

My lungs struggled to inhale. I nodded. No prince in my future now. My parents always knew how to conduct wise transactions and I felt certain this was a wise move. As the oldest daughter, I'd sacrifice my dreams for them.

Chapter 3

CHANGES BEGIN FOR THE FAMILY

My future groom came to my parents' home and we met for the first time. He took me on dates and we learned a little about each other in the weeks before the wedding.

He was twelve years older than I was but quite handsome. Though apprehensive at first, I remembered what my mother had said about security. If things were bad enough to have me marry a wealthy man this fast, their fortune might be at risk. I had to do what I could to protect my parents and all they had worked for through the years.

During my short engagement, people brought gifts on silver trays along with stacks of cash bundled for us. My parents gave me gold and diamond jewelry.

Family and friends came from far and near to attend the wedding. My friends told me that there were hundreds of cars lined up throughout the neighborhood.

After our wedding, my husband moved me, along with one adopted sister, my younger brother David, and one of their mates to Kampong Thom with him. That city was a good three-and-a-half-hour drive from Phnom Penh.

My life changed as a newlywed. I gave up my position as a spoiled daughter and took on the luxurious role of the wife of a governor. Early in our marriage, I gave birth to our son, Alex. My mother called him Piseth.

I embraced the challenge as a new wife with a young son. My husband gave me stacks of money to enjoy many privileges. I often took my sisters out shopping in the luxurious car that my husband had bought for me.

When unrest grew on the streets, about once a month we traveled in a plane or helicopter to Phnom Penh to visit my family. Though protected from the details, I became aware of how dangerous it had become for my parents.

They could no longer travel safely to take care of the rubber tree plantation. I knew it was time for their crop to produce a substantial income, but I resisted asking them such a question. If they needed money, they knew they could come to me and my husband.

Chin Seng Heang, my husband, obtained the permits for getting into the huge fishing industry around Kampong Thom and Tonle Sap. I discreetly shared some of that money to help my parents and my siblings with food and other essentials.

My husband and I visited my parents in Phnom Penh with our son when he was a couple of months old. My husband took a flight back home and I stayed with my family, planning to join him within a day or two. That night, from the hallway in their home, I heard them speaking. I heard my mother ask, "Why? I don't understand."

My father's voice shuddered. "Lon Nol had three of his soldiers pointing guns at my back. I had to read it. The whole country heard me announce over the radio that the National Assembly voted to depose Sihanouk and Lon Nol is now head of Cambodia."

Stunned, I stopped and listened from the hallway, trying to catch my breath. Pa had always been loyal to the monarchy. King Sihanouk no longer ruled? We knew the king had been visiting France earlier in the year. I thought he was still traveling to meet with heads of state, maybe in China.

I leaned my head into the room and saw Pa seated, with his head in his hands. My mother knelt at his feet. She insisted, "It's too dangerous, you must leave the country with us."

My father shook his head. "Lon Nol is now in charge. I can't leave, but you and the children must go. Our lives are in danger here."

I pulled back into the hall and covered my mouth to silence a gasp that threatened to squeak out, giving away my presence.

Years ago, right-wing supporters had elected Lon Nol, a military general, as prime minister. But Sihanouk had remained king. Now General Lon Nol was in control?

Were we about to go into war? My stomach churned as my head recalled media images of the war with North Vietnamese soldiers and the mass graves they left in their path. How could this coup have happened? We had freedom and security with the king. Why would my father have allowed it?

My mother asked my father the question as it crossed my mind.

"Emergency powers," my father answered. "He claimed he could assume emergency powers, and he did. The military who aligned with Nol are backing him. But, regardless of how it happened, it did. Now it's too dangerous for you and the children here. They will watch my every move, so I can't leave. You must leave and take the children."

I leaned against the wall to remain upright. Surely this couldn't be happening. Did my husband know?

My mother assured him with a calm voice, "No. I will not leave you here alone. None of us will. If you can't leave, we won't either. We will all die together."

Unable to bear the heartbreaking conversation any longer, I sprinted to my room and rushed to an open window for some fresh air. Outside, men I didn't recognize stood around the grounds scanning the house and land.

Guards.

Spies.

Father was right. Lon Nol already had the home under surveillance. I remembered seeing a man I didn't recognize when the driver let me out, but I thought he must have been a new employee.

Poor Pa. He had served as a judge, a senator, a diplomat, and Minister of Religion while also the CEO for a Cambodian royal newspaper. It was easy to see why they chose him to be the voice of this announcement. I imagined the scene with guns pointing at my precious father and my chin trembled.

I swiped the tears that streaked my cheeks without my permission. I would not dwell on that awful thought. This was not the time for panic.

I forced my lungs to inhale a deep breath, but my heart pounded into my throat.

King Sihanouk was deposed.

They didn't mention his son, Prince Naradipo.

What would happen to "my" prince?

My sister Thyda came to the door and I shushed her away. I didn't have the heart to tell her what was happening, much less what I thought might come to pass. She would learn soon enough.

She insisted and bounced into my room to show me her new silk sarong for temple. "Look, Srey Na." In the Cambodian tradition, rather than using our name, we called our family members by their position within the family. As the oldest daughter, I was Srey Na to my family.

When I looked at her, she stood tall and posed with her hands pressed together and then bent at the waist in a half-bow. Of course she was lovely, but I couldn't force my face into a genuine smile. I turned and looked again at the men outside.

"What's wrong?" She stepped toward me and looked out the window. "New workers? Guards? Who are they?"

I swallowed hard. My chest hammered as I tried to think of some explanation. "King Sihanouk—"

"Yes, I know, Srey Na, King Sihanouk is out of the country. Did you get a letter from the prince?"

Shaking my head, I decided to let her have another day of innocence. Besides, it was not my place to tell her. Pa and

Mom would tell us all what we needed to know in their time. "No. No letter. I am married now." Afraid my eyes had reddened, I shifted my gaze from her to out the window.

Thyda sidled beside me. "Do you miss your husband?" She slipped her arm around my waist. "Don't worry. He will be back soon."

After a few seconds she asked, "The men out there. Did Pa hire more guards? Are we in danger?"

"I don't know." I patted her hand that landed on my waist. "Pa is probably adding security to take care of us and his grandson."

She released a sigh. "Right. He's a powerful man. He might have heard of some threat and hired more guards."

I tried to remain calm while I considered some options. They could come live with me and my husband or go live on the plantation if they could make it there. It dawned on me that being married and living away from the streets of Phnom Penh, I had been sheltered from the danger here.

I managed a smile. "Your dress is beautiful. Let me see all of it."

Thyda shrugged and stepped back toward the center of the room, her arms pressed to her side. She looked toward me with the heaviness of her thoughts revealed in her stance.

"Shoulders back, Srey Da. Stand tall. You are the beautiful daughter of a powerful man. Your sister is married to a powerful man." I winked at her. "We're okay. Pa is just taking care of us." I spoke in my most convincing tone and hoped she believed my words.

I didn't.

Chapter 4

TENSION BETWEEN LON NOL AND FATHER

When I came down for dinner, I stopped at the table with the vase of roses. One of the flowers had been trimmed too short to reach the water in the vase and had now drooped. I brushed my fingers across the wilted rose and petals fell to the table.

Staring at the single limp rose, I thought of how powerless it had become when cut away from its stem and roots. The browned petals lay helpless on the table. Dead. A sinking feeling washed over me about how much I had taken for granted and how quickly everything could change for me and my family. How many of us could stand if the coup turned into a war?

Seated in the dining room, steaming bowls of samlor machu trey, a sweet and sour soup with fish, tickled my nostrils. I inhaled the fresh steamed garlic, lemongrass, celery, tamarind juice, bean sprouts, pineapple seasoned with fish sauce, and salt. Normally, that would have lightened my spirit.

Tonight, the fish head staring at me seemed a terrible omen instead of a mouthwatering delight. This delicious soup topped with fresh green herbs and hot chili pepper had lost its appeal.

My parents' pleasant faces might have fooled the rest of the family, but not me. I could see the tension in Pa's forehead and the slight tremble in Mom's hand.

The younger siblings asked about the weekend destination. "Are we going to Kampong Som to the beach?"

Before the war started and it was still safe, my older brother, Visothara, also called Scott, would have volunteered to drive the Land Rover while father drove the Volkswagen. Everyone fit into two cars whenever we went to the mountains or the beach.

I thought of my best friend who was married to Prince Norodom Chakrapong. We often stayed with them at their vacation home in the smaller town of Kiap, near Kampong Som, on the other side of "Sihanoukville."

Now every highway outside the city had become dangerous. Between bandits and roadblocks, it had become impossible to get away for the weekend or even to check our plantation. Within town, guards spied on and followed anyone who left our house. It became a challenge just to safely navigate the streets to get food from the market.

Eyes down, Pa held his lips between his teeth. Even in this uncertainty, he remained strong. Mom offered her normal sweet smile and hinted that it would be a secret.

I didn't make eye contact with her. She knew me too well. If she saw my face, she would see that something was wrong. My mind wandered while I pushed the fish Amok—steamed coconut fish in banana leaves—in front of me from one side of the dish to the other.

Thyda sat across from me explaining all the details of her new silk sarong. As far as she knew, we still lived under a monarchy and our lives had a prosperous future.

Pa and Mom gave no hint of the conversation I had overheard earlier. I had never seen Pa as broken as I had from the hallway just hours ago. Now, he seemed invincible again. Mom synchronized every aspect of the servants and the meal to perfection, as always. Our homes, businesses, and family were all safe with them.

We were all strong in our own way. Whatever came, I would do my part. Our parents had provided us with peace and happiness along with the strength to carry on the family businesses. They had given us years of carefree lives and laid the foundation for our futures.

Scott had returned from his pilot training in Thailand and brought a girlfriend, Vasitee, with him. Now a pilot with Khmer Akas Airline, I wondered if he knew about the coup yet? Would he be called to fight if war broke out here?

Would my younger brother, Frederick, be called back from his studies in France and forced to join the military?

Metrey should be too young. My heart ached at the thought of my family in danger.

My prince.

My husband, traveling. At least I had our son and we were safe here with my parents.

Perhaps the king would return soon and nothing would change. It would be as if it never happened.

Someone elbowed me.

I looked up to find Thyda's quizzical face staring at me with raised eyebrows. She looked as if she waited for me to answer her.

"What? Did I miss something?"

"I asked," she said, "if you're going to eat or just daydream about your traveling husband? Or are you dreaming of life with a prince?"

I didn't have the heart to answer truthfully, so I laughed and lifted my spoon to my mouth.

The Next Day

Many times before, I had stood in for my mother when Pa had a ceremony to attend. That day, when my father asked me to dress for a formal event, I bowed in obedience to his request without mentioning what I had heard. I knew Pa would never put me in danger.

In my room, I found something suitable. While I dressed, my sister stopped in my room and announced she would be shopping that day. "Be careful, Srey Da." I didn't usually say that and didn't want to answer questions, so I added, "Have fun. I hope you find something beautiful."

She chuckled and tossed her hair behind one shoulder, "I always am, Srey Na. I intend to find something very special. I hope you have fun at work with Pa."

I doubted it would be as fun as the previous times, but she didn't need to know that. I waved goodbye to her and added the finishing touches to my professional attire before joining Pa.

Before we got into the car, I didn't stop to visit with the mynah bird. He chatted and vroomed as if nothing were different. My father and I got in the official car sent for us, and the chauffeur took us along the usual route to the palace.

The press had covered my father extensively through the years, due to his high-level government positions. Our names and faces had often been in the news, making us easily recognized, especially in the capital, Phnom Penh.

The regular motorcade of uniformed police officers on motorcycles escorted us in front of and behind his car. Sirens blasted at every traffic stop, giving us priority to pass by while the general traffic waited.

Before today, I had always felt like royalty when the public stopped what they were doing and peered into the windows to glimpse the occupants. This time, people gathered in small groups and pointed as our motorcade passed.

My father told me briefly that we were attending a ceremony involving Lon Nol. I didn't ask about the king or the crown prince. I knew to remain silent, stay by his side, and politely greet people who spoke to us.

Inside the palace, the gorgeous furnishings seemed to have lost their former luster. The military guards all seemed stiff and on high alert.

I tried to breathe and walk normally beside Pa as if nothing were different. Adding to my tension, the heat and humidity of this time of year, before the monsoon season began, made my legs feel like lead, and my lungs had to work twice as hard to supply the oxygen I needed to get through this.

During the ceremony, Lon Nol glanced at me several times. I struggled to maintain a pleasant look. Inside I seethed, knowing what he had already forced Pa to do and wondering what he might do to our family.

The king was now exiled from Cambodia and would not be back. The words rattled in my head. That probably meant the crown prince, my prince, had been exiled with him, if not executed.

I blinked and maintained my composure, staring ahead to a random point beyond Lon Nol while he spoke. I couldn't risk humiliating Pa or bringing any suspicion to my family. Even though I looked past Lon Nol, his eyes continued to glare at me. I remained composed on the outside. I couldn't risk causing trouble for Pa.

Chapter 5

FAMILY ADDITIONS—ORPHANS ADOPTED

That evening, my sister slipped into my room before dinner and whispered that she had been followed on her shopping trip. She had also heard rumors about Lon Nol and the king.

I could no longer hide the truth from her. I sat on the bed and patted the space beside me, inviting her to sit. After I told her what I knew, she leaned against me and sobbed.

I hugged her. "Srey Da, we must be strong for our parents. It's okay to cry in front of me, but they need us to be strong. They will take care of us. You'll see. Everything will be okay."

She sniffled and nodded before she stood.

"Now go, get ready to eat. Pa and Mom will tell us what we need to do when we need to know."

She squeezed me and wiped her face before she left my room. I looked out my window and watched a guard looking directly at my window. He maintained a stern face and held his weapon in a ready position. I stepped back and drew in a full breath, steadying myself to face my family for dinner.

When I passed the Buddha statue in the hall, I found a fresh bouquet in front of it. Probably Mom placed it there or asked a housekeeper to do it. She knew how much we would need any blessing available.

We usually kept the conversation light during meals, but after the dinner bell sounded, my siblings gathered outside the dining room in a feverish meeting. "Srey Na, tell us what you know. Srey Da was followed and even our staff was followed when they shopped for groceries at the market. Have you heard the king has been deposed?"

I raised my hands to slow down the questions. "Yes. He is in exile. The guards are from Lon Nol."

I didn't have to say more. Their wide eyes told me of their fear.

Motioning to the dining room, I said, "Come, let's go eat and honor our parents with the respect they deserve."

My parents smiled and welcomed us to the table. Though we had never before discussed politics at the table, Mom gradually introduced the topic. "I know some of you traveled today. Are you all okay? Did anything happen?"

Once my sister told the family about her experience, others opened up about being followed as well as the rumors they heard. I watched Pa's strong eyes become tender as he listened to the danger around us. How had I not noticed the lines around his eyes?

Mom inquired, "Did anyone threaten you?"

"Oh, no. At least not directly," someone answered.

I didn't mention the armed guard outside my room.

Someone asked about leaving the city and going to the beach or the plantation for a getaway.

Pa and Mom shook their heads. Pa explained, "I am required to stay here."

Mom added, "And we will stay by your father. We are a family and we will be together, no matter what."

We heard people walking down the hall and silenced the conversation until they passed out of hearing range. My parents had rented the front part of our massive home to some Korean pilots who came to the city when the demand for pilots increased. One pilot brought his teenage daughter, Wendy. I smiled and nodded to her as she and her father passed by the doorway.

The topics during the remainder of our meal remained light and hopeful. We all needed a little hope.

Cambodia might have lost its soul, but my parents had always demonstrated compassion and generosity even to those we didn't know. Our cook told us of three children who had been orphaned after a B-52 bomb took their parents' lives. With no organized orphanages in Cambodia before the war, Pa and Mom immediately brought the two boys and one girl, ages four, five, and seven, to be our adopted siblings. They went from nine children to twelve in one day. The youngsters brought happiness to our family, even though they came to us through a great tragedy.

We became protective of our adopted siblings. I refused to allow anyone to call them anything other than my brothers and sister, and certainly no hurtful names. None of us felt threatened by the addition of our new siblings. Our parents treated us all the same.

* * *

Before Lon Nol's regime, we had often entertained on the spacious first floor of our home, which accommodated a live band with plenty of room for dancing, plus seating. Any older guests would join our parents on the third floor on the sky balcony. My father liked to show off the beautiful orchids he grew there.

Now, fearful to leave our home for anything other than a necessity, on some evenings when the spies were gone, we invited our neighbors over to watch TV with us. The television provided only background noise though. We discussed the new government and the distressing rumors of a communist cleansing of all those who might oppose the new regime. Theories ran rampant about what might happen next.

After I had Alex settled in his bed, I mingled with the others for a while. Then I met Scott, who had returned from his copilot flight. He pressed one finger against his mouth and motioned for me to come back into Alex's room. My son was sleeping so deeply he didn't notice when Scott took Alex's wrist and placed it over his forehead, like a worried old man. I tried not to laugh too loudly and wake Alex.

Scott motioned other family members in and showed them how funny little Alex looked with his hand draped across his head, then he crossed one leg over the other. We laughed until we had to leave the room. Oh, how I loved my family.

I said goodnight to my parents and siblings and tried to sleep. The house became still and quiet. The tension of the day rested between my shoulders, and I cringed a little as I tossed in the bed, trying to find sleep. I told myself I was safe under my father's roof and needed to rest for whatever tomorrow brought. I had to be strong for my family, my son.

Instead, my thoughts kept niggling at me about why my husband hadn't called yet to let me know he arrived safely.

Around four in the morning, I went up to the top balcony for fresh air and lay on a bench to look at the beautiful night sky. A bright light with a long tail, maybe two hundred feet long, appeared in the sky above me and seemed to nearly touch my brother's bedroom on top of the balcony. Something about it unnerved me, and I went back down to sleep near my son.

I passed by the flower vase again. They had no more water and all bowed, lifeless in the vase. I held Alex and snuggled with him. I squelched the tears that puddled in my eyes. My husband was out there somewhere. After all the discussions of war with our family friends, I shuddered and wished he were here, with us.

We were safe for the moment, but for how long?

Chapter 6

WAR COMES TO PHNOM PENH—FAMILY FLEES

I woke with the feeling of falling and clenched the bed for dear life. The three-story house shook. I blinked, clearing my eyes, and I pinched my leg. I was not dreaming.

Lights from outside the window flickered in multiple colors dancing around my room. A massive barrage of explosions as strong as thunder and lightning rattled us again, but this was no thunderstorm.

I found my way to the window. Gunfire and bombs lit up the sky. A continual series of explosions rattled the windows and filled the room with eerie dancing lights.

With the light from the explosions, I could see the entire city, but everything in it was pitch black, like a ghost town. No lights from homes or even traffic lights. I heard scrambling from the others inside our home, but a deadly quiet hovered over the city.

No business activity.

The stillness of fear hung over the city with the clouds of smoke and debris. My heartbeat sounded like thunder in my ears against the thick silence.

The bombs came from in front, behind, and all around us. My heart pounded harder. Faster. Sulfur drifted in through the window along with the acrid smoke.

I grabbed my son and found my parents and the others. We all huddled in fear as the nightmare outside welled up in us. How could anything be left of the city after that?

Pa spoke up. "Let's get under the staircase. And bring all the silver items—such as big bowls, trays, plates, silverware, and more—to hide in a pillowcase under the staircase as well."

Mom said, "Bring what you can stuff into a bag—small valuables in case . . ."

I sprinted to my room and gathered a few things for Alex, my cash, the jewelry I had with me, and followed everyone back downstairs. We gathered under the first-floor staircase to have the most protection. We sat tightly together with a stack of silver in the corner. None of our lights worked. I picked up a phone, but it was dead too.

If this is how my life would end, I was thankful I had married and had already borne a son. My husband had flown back to Kampong Thom. If the bombing was only in Phnom Penh, he should be okay. He might come and get us.

Scott's girlfriend had traveled back to Thailand. She should be okay, too, but might not be able to get to us if the border closed. Too many possibilities to consider amid the unknown. I stroked the hair of my precious son and whispered in his ear how much I loved him.

We huddled behind the staircase for hours, hoping everything would calm down before sunrise. We all looked to one another for answers. When one of my sisters would look at me, I would smile and mouth, "We're okay."

Inside, my stomach churned as I thought about whether or not I would ever see my husband again or be able to protect Alex from the deadly evil exploding around us.

The noises settled, but when the light of dawn came through some windows, we heard gunfire, rockets, and bloodcurdling screams—cries of people calling for help from every direction near our house. Desperate pleas.

By noon we slowly came out from under the stairway, one by one. We made our way to the windows and got a glimpse of the panic and devastation in a city now covered in gray dust. I picked up a phone again but still no dial tone. Scott and I got so nervous for our loved ones and didn't know how to find them. I had no way to reach my husband nor Scott his girlfriend. They would come and find us—if they could.

Throngs of people were on the streets, fleeing the city in cars and on foot. Everyone traveled in the same direction, away from the inner city, into the countryside.

A huge military truck rumbled behind the crowd and past our home. Heavily armed people stood in the back wearing black uniforms with red scarves shouting from bullhorns. "You must leave now. Evacuate the city immediately. Leave now." Some lifted their weapons and shot toward the sky; others pointed them at the crowds. They each had multiple ammo belts and guns, ready for battle.

The screeching sounds of the horns and sirens blasted our ears even louder than the screams of my terrified son. I had no way to speak comforting words to him louder than the chaos. We had to leave. I would soothe him when we reached safety.

When one of my siblings slowed, I nodded for them to move forward or jolted them from their trance by pulling on their arms. I shared their compassion, but this was not the time for gawking or crying. We had to take action.

Mom told us, "Bring whatever you can stuff into a small bag. Small valuables, clothes. Hurry."

I gathered the things I put together for myself and Alex. We all packed a few belongings into three cars and my minibike and joined the frantic crowds on the street. The nightmare became more intense outside. The usually lush green tropical landscape had been covered with gray soot. No birds called out. Only weary shell-shocked people weeping and sirens blasting. I saw flames and smoke from the city buildings we had passed just the day before.

Intense smoke rose from the south part of the city where the poor lived in shack homes. What had happened to our beautiful city?

I pulled a light scarf over Alex's face to keep out some of the smoke and ash. My heart wanted to pour out the grief over what I saw, but my mouth could not find words to speak.

People swarmed the streets, weaving in and around heavy traffic. Frustrated drivers blasted their horns. The frenzy to get out before more bombing began grew more frantic every moment.

Our family group stayed together and headed north, toward my home. Our best chance seemed to be to get into the countryside to our north, and if possible, to my husband and home in Kampong Thom.

We inched out of the city among the thousands of other devastated people. Most held cloths over their mouths to filter the stench of the bombs and smoke.

Gunfire, smoke, and terror filled the city. The able-bodied people pulled along the bloodied and injured. Stumbling children clung to adults trying to keep pace. Dazed husbands sheltered their wives with one arm around their shoulders. They constantly scanned for signs of danger or perhaps another escape route. Some yelled out a name, trying to locate a loved one.

With people flowing out of every building, all life was draining from Phnom Penh. No businesses open. No electricity. Only fear and panic.

When we neared the northern edge of the city, we heard another blast. Putrid black smoke rose in slow motion from the Esso oil storage facility in front of us. I swiped angry tears into the grit already on my face and focused on an escape route. I had to remain strong to get my son and family out of here.

Because of Pa's political reputation, we knew that he would be targeted by the new government. Mom clung to him.

Weary crowds dispersed into the fields, abandoning cars that ran out of gas.

Eventually, our vehicles also ran out of gas. We siblings had grouped together keeping an eye on our parents but kept a little distance just in case we needed to scramble for safety.

Some people who recognized my father took us across the river to Prek Tamer. We had to leave all of our cars on the main road, and all we could take with us was my very favorite Japanese bicycle. That night, we sheltered in a field and built a small fire for light. We had built so many fires for fun evenings in a cottage on our plantation. Tonight we had no cottage. No workers came to bring us what we needed.

I allowed my heart a moment to grieve over the reality I had hoped was only a nightmare. Perhaps the devastation had been limited to Phnom Penh. If we could reach Kampong Thom, my family could shelter there with me and my husband. He had to be worried. We had talked about Lon Nol and his semi-presidential government that resembled more of a military dictatorship. He knew the risks but was accustomed to being able to deal with political figures and businessmen. The Khmer Rouge did not seem to be negotiating or dealing.

I stared at the stars I had seen so many times from the balcony of our home. Bright and clear, they must not know of our heartache here. God, help me. Help us. Even though I didn't know of the Christian God, in the extreme chaos I was pleading for help from the highest power I could imagine.

The silent stars gave me no answer. At least they provided a little light in the heavy darkness. Without the blazing heat from the sun, the temperature dropped into the seventies with a light breeze. Even with such a pleasant temperature, I felt a chill, like fingers of death clawing toward us.

I clenched my jaw.

Fear would not rule me.

Gunshots startled me, and I caught my breath. I had to remain focused. I alternated between moments of safety with an overwhelming sense of doom.

Any rustle in the bushes brought us to alert and we froze to utter stillness, even holding our breath as long as possible. Another group of evacuees cried out in the distance. The danger must be in their camp. I nestled Alex to me and sang softly to him. Exhausted, he went to sleep in my arms. The stars emerged overhead, as the smoke lifted. Silence again refreshed us.

Mom suggested we pretend we were on the sky balcony after a long party. My brothers joined in and reminisced about parties they had—the music, the food, the dancing. Their voices faded after a while. I let them fantasize but realized we might never again have a party. Where would we find food?

My sleep-deprived brain fell into a trance and brought me to a dream: the memory of sleeping at the beach house of my best friend at Kiap. On a mountain just across the street from the beach, we hiked a trail that led down, across the street from the house, and took us through beautiful gardens and out onto a pier.

At the end of the pier stood a small cottage with stairs leading down to the sea. The waves lapped in a steady rhythm at the base of the cottage. We played with the waves during the day. We watched hundreds of tiny, colorful jellyfish floating in the water. Some of them looked like small octopuses—almost like lotus flowers floating next to the pier. I remembered the calmness of the sea during the day and then its liveliness and turbulence at night.

At that beautiful retreat, the sun didn't stop us from playing for long hours even when its rays baked our skin. A nearby market sold fresh-cooked blue crab and freshly cooked cakes wrapped in banana leaves.

The dream was so real, I reached out my hand to take the food and the movement woke me. The beach was only a wishful vision. My family huddled in the darkness somewhere outside the city, with no hope of rescue in sight.

As other refugees settled near us for the night, we heard them say the communist militia had taken complete control of Phnom Penh.

King Sihanouk had long spoken of the dangers of a Khmer Rouge. If red communist flags now waved over the capital Phnom Penh, did that mean they had the entire country?

Even though my family clustered around me, with no way to reach my husband, I felt alone. I looked to the stars again. Where was my husband? Where was Scott's girlfriend? Did the world know what had happened here? To us? Would anyone come and help us?

With no answer, I looked back to the city to the south of us and watched the smoke billow from the city that was once my home.

Chapter 7

FLEEING THE ENEMY—DEPRIVATION BEGINS

Hunger rumbled within me, but safety had to be our priority. Military patrols came along the roadways and our faces would no doubt be among those targeted by the new regime. Under the cover of darkness, we walked, heading north, away from Phnom Penh. Mom and I took turns holding Alex. We found fruit now and then to curb our hunger pangs.

I could not tell how many others surrounded us. Likely, several thousand people. Some on foot, others in vehicles, all wore blank, tearstained faces.

In the morning, we gathered our things and walked in cadence under the searing light of the hot sun, occasionally wiping the sweat from our faces. We had to keep moving.

Day after day we continued until the sun set over the mountains. At dusk, we searched for any tiny suitable spot to cook whatever we brought with us, and whatever we found along our way. Others also staked out places to stay for the night and small fires flickered around us. We used any flat area near the street for our beds, and any wooded area for our bathrooms.

Tired, hungry, and thirsty, without a destination, everyone put one foot in front of the other, using every last drop of adrenaline. As the imminent danger passed, a few groups at a time split off in different directions to find rest, food, and shelter. We gathered edible greens along the road and pathways to have something to eat. The communists might have wanted us to die of starvation, but God provided in nature enough for us to survive.

We walked and ran for about three weeks. There were no places open to shop, no hotels. When we found currency littering the streets, we realized it had been nationalized and no longer had any value.

Now and then, someone succumbed to their injuries on the journey and died. Families wept and tried to bury their dead before they rejoined the march to safety. In the mass of people, we saw one of my father's distant relatives, a radio news reporter, who had become separated from his wife and his children. Several weeks later we found him dead inside an empty shed that we had sought for shelter.

Beyond exhausted, we came to a little village along the Tonle Mekong River, but away from the main road. There, in Akar Kong, no one seemed to recognize us. My father used a piece of jewelry to purchase a small section of land. It was only a tiny spot, but large enough for us to build a shelter to protect us from the coming monsoon season and to hide from soldiers. My father and brothers used bamboo and straw to build a small hut with enough space for us all to sleep in.

I remembered the spies at my parents' house and realized that if the new government found us, we would be labeled as a threat to them because of Pa's loyalty to the monarchy. Other walking refugees told us the police in Phnom Penh had been rounded up and executed in the Olympic stadium.

After dark, I scavenged the nearby area for food for the family. Each night I returned with whatever I could find. The grief on Pa's face when I returned with some rice, fruit, and berries told me how deeply his pride suffered. "Pa, don't worry. We can always find our way to the plantation and live off the farm there."

"You don't understand." He shook his head. "The situation is worse than you knew. Lately, we've only had supplies in Phnom Penh delivered by small planes and helicopters. We hoped General Lon Nol's military could hold off the Khmer Rouge, but recently several thousand more Khmer Rouge troops surrounded the city. Today, they overtook the local police.

"Because of the bombing along the border and our military having such trouble with the Khmer Rouge, I haven't been able to get to the plantation in quite some time. It hasn't been maintained or fertilized. I hired planes to dust them for a while." He shook his head. "Now, when it should be producing hundreds of barrels of sap, I doubt if we even own it anymore." His voice cracked and he sat up straighter before he continued. "They've already nationalized the banks and the currency. I expect Khmer Rouge will nationalize all businesses if they haven't already." He stared ahead.

"But, Pa. Surely there is something we can do. You know so many people, powerful people."

"Those people are no longer powerful. I didn't want you to worry, but Sihanouk has fled to China. Prince Naradipo has disappeared."

"Is he alive?"

My father lifted his shoulders and shook his head. "We knew him as 'Prince of the People.' Now, they are calling him 'The Most Unfortunate Prince.'"

I sat silent for a few moments next to the strongest man I knew. Wealthy, brilliant, and powerful, now helpless.

While our hopes drifted away somewhere in the darkness, I watched Mom as she broke off bite-sized pieces of a ripe pear for Alex. "Pa—"

What could I tell him?

I took in a breath and told him, "Pa, we'll be okay. You have always provided for us. We'll find a way." I had to preserve some of his dignity and will to survive. "We have to, for Alex."

He patted my knee and glanced up at his grandson and wife. "We will survive. We will find a way." Looking at me he added, "You are the oldest daughter and are already showing me how strong and capable you are. Eat, so you can keep your strength, daughter. You will need it."

I nodded. "I will do whatever it takes, Pa. You know I will." I walked over to sit with my mom and Alex. My son raised his hands for me to hold him, and I obliged.

Mom said, "He liked the pear."

I nodded. Alex wriggled under my shirt to nurse. He looked up at me and his eyes smiled.

I squeezed him a little tighter. "You are such a good boy. You will have so many wonderful things. Mom will see to it."

I kissed his forehead as I rocked him lightly. "I promise, Alex. I promise."

I couldn't restrain the tear that slipped from my eye. It dripped onto his forehead and he reached up to touch the wet spot. I pressed my lips together for a moment, repressing a sob. "We're okay, sweetheart. We're going to be okay."

Mom grabbed my hand. "I need to tell you something."

"What is it? Are you okay?" The lines on her face told of the deep concern she had for our family. We all worried that Pa would be killed along with my two older brothers, Scott and Metrey. Scott, a pilot, and Metrey, a pharmacist, would both be valuable to the Khmer Rouge army. If they were found, they would be forced to serve or be killed.

Mom nodded. "I'm okay. I just wanted you to know that not long after you married, I found a business opportunity." She looked around to see if anyone else could hear before she continued. "I own a gem mine."

My mother, an entrepreneur. Her eyes held a sparkle I hadn't seen recently. "Mom . . ." I started, but I didn't know what to ask first.

While Alex's nursing slowed and he drifted into a blissful sleep, she huddled near me and answered the most obvious question: *when?* "When it became too dangerous for the family of a government official to travel, we became unable to work the plantation and rice field."

"Yes, I know."

She raised one shoulder and said, "In Krong Pailin, no one knew me." She winked. "I bought a gemstone mine there and a friend helped me take care of it."

I tried to remember Krong Pailin. "North, near the Thai border?"

She nodded. "They are known for their abundant supply of rubies, sapphires, and emeralds. We had been selling them across the border to Thailand."

"You are amazing, Mom." I held such admiration for this smart and strong woman. I hoped I would live long enough to be like her. Honored that she shared this with me, I smiled at my lovely mother and kept her secret. I didn't want to get anyone's hopes up. When Mom wanted anyone else to know, she would tell them.

Because of the malnourishment and stress, my body reacted by stopping my milk production. When Alex cried in hunger, my mom recognized what had happened. She told me to gather a few of the smallest ears of corn from a nearby field when I went to look for food that day. When I brought the tiny ears back, she boiled them. Alex sucked baby corn juice as a replacement for milk. I was so thankful to be able to give him something to soothe his hunger.

Now and then, I saw someone who resembled my husband or heard a voice that was similar to his. Every time, I was disappointed to learn it wasn't him. Was he alive? Injured? I had no means to tell him of our location. I prayed, "God, keep him safe." Every blistering day and lonely night I felt a little less hopeful.

I watched Scott look at every young woman with a small child who resembled his girlfriend and their son. I'm sure his heart broke every time he realized it wasn't her. Each day we both looked with hope, but away from the main road, we saw fewer people. Our hearts ached to find those we loved.

We lived in continual fear and had dwindling hope of being reunited with them, but at least most of us were together.

Weeks passed and we fell into a routine. Mom's smile returned and Pa walked outside now and then, visiting with the villagers. Perhaps we could eventually make it to a place with better opportunities.

Chapter 8

CAPTURED—INJURED BY KHMER ROUGE SOLDIER

After several weeks, we felt secure enough that I could go out during the day and exchange whatever valuables we had for food among the friendly villagers.

My younger brother found a net and occasionally caught fish from a small stream. My mother gathered wild edible greens from the field next to our shed. Both brothers, Scott and Metrey, used their talents to repair wristwatches for the Khmer Rouge soldiers in exchange for food to support us.

At dusk, the people went inside to get ready for bed, so I returned to our hut with the food I had found for the family along empty streets.

Mom waited for me as usual near the doorway and opened her mouth to speak. Before she could, something rammed against the back of my neck. I tried to keep my balance, but the blow threw me to the ground, dazed.

While dust swirled around me, I anchored my palms on the dirt and gravel to steady the world spinning around me. Someone slammed me with something hard over and over. I focused on remaining conscious. My mother's voice faded into the distance, screaming for help and pleading with my attacker to stop hitting me.

When one blow turned me over, I saw my attacker. A man dressed in a black uniform with a cap on his head. Khmer Rouge. He smirked and raised the butt of his rifle above me for another hit, but kicked me instead. He walked away, leaving me bloodied and bruised in the street.

Mom helped me to our hut and questioned me as she cleaned me up. I assured my distraught family that other than my neck, I thought I was okay. I lightly touched the tender spot and wondered how my head didn't fall off after the impact of the rifle butt. I shrugged my shoulders. "I'll survive."

My head and neck ached through the night. I battled nausea but finally drifted into a light sleep while my family whispered in the dark. I dreamed we were vacationing again in the mountains. I thought in my dream, *We must be at Phnom Bokor, which is higher than Phnom Kirirom, with deeper valleys and steeper hills.* At the other side, I saw the freshwater streams flowing over the giant flat rocks. Peaceful. Beautiful. Refreshing. I felt the cool mountain breeze on my arms and inhaled the fragrance of the rumduol flowers. It seemed like a hundred years before, when I walked through gardens where their blooms greeted everyone with their sweet perfume.

I looked for the local Japanese farmer who always had the freshest watercress and tomatoes. That would taste so good right now. When I turned around and looked farther away at the peak of the mountain above the tall trees, I saw a white cloud swirling in a circle from the strong air around the top.

My head nodded to one side, reactivating my neck injury and bringing me back to reality. I woke and grabbed my neck to stop the sharp pain. My family still chatted in whispers, but I was no longer on a mountain retreat. A single stem of rumduol lay in the corner, wilting. Mom must have found it.

Heaving a sigh, I snuggled Alex to me. "I will always be here for you, my son. I will protect you until my dying breath."

The next morning, I was stiff and bruised, but I insisted I could go out for food. I would not let one bully of a soldier keep me from doing all I could to support my family.

My parents told my sixteen-year-old brother, Rick, to go with me as I traded for food. I agreed. That was probably a good idea.

A few months ago, I would not have set foot outside our home without being clad in the most fashionable clothing and my long hair perfectly combed. Now, survival was utmost on my mind so that I could get my son out of this darkness.

We stayed in the same village for a few months. Now and then we talked about our home and whether it might be safe there. Every day I wondered about my husband and prayed he was safe so that Alex and I could return to him soon. If it was still too dangerous in Phnom Penh, perhaps my family could all stay with us. Perhaps the communists would be defeated and our king could return.

* * *

The cool, rainy season had begun. After scavenging for food one day, I slogged through the mud to my family hut. Each family member was seated, but unusually sad. I saw Mom, Alex, and each of my brothers and sisters, but couldn't find Pa.

My hands perspired as I searched for him, and my heartbeat quickened. "Where is Pa?"

No one answered. I searched for some sign on someone's face, but no one looked at me. "Where is Pa? What has happened? Why won't you tell me?"

When Mom lifted her head, I saw her reddened eyes. With more courage than anyone else in the room, she answered my question. "A soldier came in with your Pa's picture from the newspaper in his hand. He screamed at everyone, pointing to the picture, 'Kuy Peou, Kuy Peou.' Then they took him." She lifted her face to look at the bamboo ceiling. "They took him, away."

My heart struggled to maintain a steady rhythm. I looked around in unbelief, hoping against hope to find him in a shadow somewhere.

I had never lived without him. I felt so helpless and alone. How could my world exist without my father or my husband?

The pelting rain outside felt like the world wept with us. I trembled without knowing what to say. Devastated and heartbroken, we all sobbed through the darkness of the night.

A chill engulfed me again. We had found a discarded empty bag that had once held three hundred pounds of rice. When I lived in Kampong Thom, merchants stuffed the empty rice bags with bundles of cash stacked on top of one another and brought them to my husband to be deposited in the bank.

I never dreamed I would have to use a rice bag as cover from the night air and rain. I sighed as I patted the empty bag into place over my legs. It seemed rather fitting that I used something so utterly empty when I felt just as empty.

Mom sat alone in the darkness. Silent. Stoic.

Only the sounds of the insects and an occasional sob disturbed the heavy night air. Perhaps the morning light will bring some hope to our lives. Maybe they will bring Pa back. We only have to get through the night.

* * *

The next day, and for many days after that, while I searched for food I also searched for Pa everywhere I could. Beginning every sunrise, I looked, hoping to get a glimpse of him or meet someone who knew where he was while I exchanged goods for food throughout the day.

Of everyone I asked, no one had seen him, and no one knew where he was. Thousands of people were missing, and now one of them was my father. None of us knew where they might be, but we held on to a little hope of finding them.

A few months later, soldiers made an announcement to everyone from the city park to get ready to take the train. The Khmer Rouge must have lived among the original villagers, because they seemed never to border them. Only people from the city were leaving by train, headed toward the Thai border to Battambang. The armed soldiers yelled at us to get ready and then demanded we leave our hut and go to board the train.

How would Pa find us? Would my husband ever find me and Alex? We scurried to pack our meager belongings into sacks. I held Alex in one arm and a bag across my shoulder when the soldiers herded us to the train station and into an old-fashioned train. We didn't recognize any of the passengers. We stood, packed in side by side, with no room to move.

The train chugged into motion, moving much slower than most trains of that time. We had no food to eat. I looked at Mom. She had always been so prepared, so calm. Brokenness hung on her like a heavy shawl.

The train occasionally stopped in the fields or jungles so people could sleep on the ground and go to the bathroom in the woods. We had no idea where we were. No visible landmarks from the windows, only the countryside. There was no one to rescue us. I held my son and remembered how his father looked forward to doing things with Alex. The hope of ever seeing him dripped away every passing day.

Helpless and stranded in the wilderness, we had to have been at least five hundred miles away from home.

The train stopped every night so we could get out and sleep. The most I hoped for was rest. My empty stomach gnawed and I pressed against the pain with my crossed arms. Between the hunger pangs and worry, my eyes only closed for a few minutes at a time. My mother checked on each of us and offered some comfort. Under any other circumstance, she and Pa would have provided tables filled with food. Her sorrow-filled eyes broke my heart. We were five hundred miles away from home, from Pa and my husband.

Somewhere on the outskirts of Battambang city, the train stopped in a lovely small village. After endless days of viewing only the countryside, it was so nice to see beautiful streets lined with inviting homes. The area had enchanting scenery full of trees and flowers. If we were to settle here, we could manage quite well.

As the soldiers ushered the hundreds of passengers off the train, the villagers welcomed us with giant open pots of cooked food. After long months without real food, eating real meat and vegetables felt like a wedding feast. Months of starvation made us more than thankful to God for this meal from heaven.

My brothers ate full plates of food and went back for more. I felt such pain for them when I saw how hungry Scott and Metrey were.

Not long before we evacuated Phnom Penh, my brother Scott had reminded me of how handsome he would look in his pilot's uniform with a pilot's cap on his head. That day we reminisced about the day when he had landed in Kampong Thom and stopped by my house while on break. I prepared lunch for us of homemade sausages. He reminded me that sausages were his favorite food. While my hands were busy with preparations, he had sweetly kissed my head. We had no idea how soon we would be so hungry.

The generous townspeople provided enough food for us all to be fed until we were full. We could not thank God enough for the people in the village and the meal they provided. We thanked the villagers many times for cooking and sharing with us and for their benevolence toward us.

The following day, when the guards didn't allow us to wander into the town, we realized our journey didn't end in that kindly village.

Chapter 9

FORCED LABOR—BROTHERS PLAN ESCAPE

The soldiers forced us away from the village and into the rice fields. They told us the old ways were gone. Our new leader, Pol Pot, ordered everyone to work to provide food for what he called Democratic Kampuchea. Our jobs would now be in the fields. The soldiers followed everyone who appeared to wander off from the group and shouted sharp warnings to anyone who didn't obey orders immediately.

My parents owned rice fields and I had spent time there. I remembered how during the growing season, lush, green rice bushes covered the fields. After the harvest, piles of rice hay remained, somehow making the fields look even larger.

Back then, the fields had been enchanting to me, in a rustic way. The well at our rice field held a special fascination. It was different from the hand-pump well at the plantation. It was the older type, surrounded by a circular wall and covered with a small roof. To access the water, workers used a crank and a bucket. Something about it seemed old-fashioned and quaint.

Now, the idea of working to own property or earn a living seemed so far away. The country of Cambodia under Pol Pot felt nothing like the Cambodia I had known and loved. Under King Sihanouk, we had been free to buy and sell as we liked. We could worship and pursue education in any way we chose.

Now, we were at the mercy of Pol Pot's soldiers. They led us into a vast open field and separated us into different age groups. Teenagers were usually sent to work far away from the adults. In the middle of nowhere, we arrived in a "deadly zone," sometimes referred to as the "killing fields." The nearest village, Chong Chadour, was far away. Only the soldiers knew where we were, and they could do with us as they wished.

Several shacks built above the ground with rice straw roofs and bamboo walls dotted the area designated to us. The house had no kitchen or bathroom. Each hut had enough room for a small family to lie down at night to sleep. They sheltered our family from the rain and the hot sun, but that was all.

The Khmer Rouge soldiers surrounded us. The soldiers watched everyone, pointing, talking to one another, and laughing at times. In essence, we were their slaves. They had control over every aspect of our lives and disobedience brought punishment or death. We were their captives and completely helpless to do anything about it.

At sunrise, they ordered us into the rice fields. Bent over, we sloshed in the mud to gather the rice ready for harvest and plant more slips of rice plants. Leeches sucked on our legs. Birds swooped over us, hoping to catch bugs.

After a couple of weeks in the deadly zone, we reached Chong Chadour, where soldiers ordered us to work in a rice field. When we arrived, the rice appeared to be in the first stages of growth and leaves had begun to sprout. They grew strong, healthy, and green—very close to each other. Once they were more than a foot tall, they had to be replanted with extra space for better production.

On the first day in the rice field, after a couple of hours, because of the dense, thick green leaves, it became hard to see the ground underneath. The ground was moist but not wet. So instead of bending down and pulling the small rice shoots, everyone sat on the dirt.

Just before our meal break, my hand touched something huge and pliable while I pulled the plants. When I looked closer under those bushes, I saw a huge snake sleeping next to me, and I was the only one who could see it. It may have been around three or four yards long and curved in a long zigzag under the thick green bushes. I was so scared I jumped away from it, screaming for help. Everybody around me stood, and the Khmer Rouge soldiers and leaders watching us ran toward me.

I pointed to it, near hysteria. A soldier grabbed it and yanked it away from the bushes. He kept pulling more of the snake into the open. When we finally saw the entire length of the snake, he slapped it on the ground several times, killing it. After it stopped moving, they laughed about it; they took it with them to prepare for cooking and ate it. I was glad it didn't bite me, but my heart pounded for a long time afterward.

In the evening, they gave us a spoonful of watery rice for our food ration. Surely, someone would rescue us soon.

I prayed quietly so the soldiers didn't realize what I was doing. Pol Pot had ordered all religion outlawed and we weren't allowed any discussions of God. We were told the government would now provide for us. They expected us to never question the government. It seemed they wanted us to shift from thinking for ourselves and worshipping, to mindless obedience to this new god of Khmer Rouge.

In the mornings that followed, we found grieving families whose loved ones had been taken away by the Khmer Rouge during the night. The sadness and shock were evident on their faces, but the soldiers reprimanded anyone who cried aloud. Any signs of compassion brought their stern disapproval.

When we worked in the fields, away from the soldiers' hearing, I learned that men, mostly, had been taken, raising deep concern for my brothers.

At first, we didn't understand how the danger had escalated for educated adult males and females older than twenty years old. The Khmer Rouge soldiers were suspicious of everyone with higher education, a wealthy background, a military connection, or a business or government background. Those who had a handsome appearance earned extra supervision. A few at a time, they disappeared during the night.

The teenagers, including our three younger brothers Rick, Notch, and Nong (David), were divided into different groups and sent away from us.

Those of us who remained worked under the blazing heat and hoped for a few morsels of rice before we collapsed in our shack at night.

For several weeks after we first arrived, one of the soldiers often went out of his way to speak to me. He was so kind and friendly. One evening, he sneaked into the shack where I slept alone. I didn't know what his intentions were, but my brothers Metrey and Scott feared that this soldier wanted to harm me. They made a lot of noise to protect me, and he fled. My brothers saved me more than once. I was so grateful to have them.

The daily disappearances of adult males continued for months. Metrey and Scott came to me one day. Metrey told me, "Srey Na. They will come and take us like they have all the other young men."

I looked at Scott, who nodded in agreement.

Scott said, "Wouldn't it be better for us to try to escape now, rather than be taken for execution?"

"Don't say that." I covered my ears.

Scott pulled my hands away from my head. "Srey Na. You are not blind or deaf. You know what is happening. We can't sit here and wait for it to happen to us."

I protested. "The soldiers might keep you for your watch repair skills." It sounded good in my head but seemed more in the category of "wishful thinking" once spoken.

They both shook their heads at me. Metrey spoke. "Mom has already lost hope of us all staying together. If we can make it to the Thai border, maybe we can find Scott's girlfriend. If we stay here, we will die."

It would be a chance. A tiny chance. If they made it, they might be able to get help for us or find Pa and my husband. I didn't want to lose them. But, I understood their willingness to die trying to live rather than wait to have their lives taken.

We all hugged as never before. My brothers left without telling me specific details about their plans. One day, they were just gone.

Though I hoped they were finding their way to Thailand, in the field, a worker told me that the explosions we heard at night were land mines exploding. The Khmer Rouge had buried them around the perimeter to prevent escapes.

My heart sank. Even if they made it past the soldiers, had they stepped on a land mine? Were they lying out there somewhere wounded and bleeding with no one to help them?

I scanned the field. Birds circled in the distance. They always did, I reminded myself. This time, I had a nauseating feeling about why they were there.

My heart ached to know about them, but there was no way to find out. My hopes of Scott and Metrey escaping their deaths and perhaps bringing help for us seemed like vapors evaporating in the sun.

If I could just have told them of my gratitude for saving my life. If only I could have said a proper goodbye.

* * *

We received food for lunch and dinner in two bowls. One contained gruel made of water with a few grains of boiled rice. The second bowl contained a salty soup with a tiny fish with a wild vegetable called trakoun, or wild water grass.

For days and months, we survived on that meager ration while performing hard labor in the tropical heat and muddy contaminated water. Desperately hungry, and hopelessly desperate, we transformed into walking skeletons. We labored mindlessly, listening for the sound of a whistle that signaled us to form a line for our rest. At least the broth helped quench a little of our thirst.

Some people decided to forage for more food in the remaining daylight. Anything moving was fair game. Field mice and rats added some protein to our diets when we could catch them.

I found a hole just the size for a good field rat and reached inside. It bit me, but someone else determined to pull it out. They were a challenge to skin and prepare, but it was the size of a chicken thigh. I saw people roast rats on a long stick over an open fire, and it had provided them with more hope than I realized.

The hunger was terrible, and the isolation added to the demoralizing situation. We couldn't visit the other camps or the neighboring village without a permission letter from the leader. Our only option was to cling to any hope, any food source we could find.

As we worked the fields, we all shared our hopes that someone would come and rescue us from the Khmer Rouge. America was such a powerful nation. We hoped they would come to rescue us. We daydreamed that somehow, someone would save us from the constant torture and slow death.

Sickness, disease, and viral infections spread throughout our camp. One of my adopted brothers died from starvation while we waited for rescue. He was only one of many. Often, in the morning, families would bring the corpses of their relatives outside their shack, to be buried.

The Khmer Rouge allowed families to bury their dead but always warned us that strength was desirable and sympathy was weakness. Any sign of weakness of mind, including religion, had to be eliminated. Execution proved to be the elimination of choice.

Any mourning or prayers had to be in silence, within our shacks.

Chapter 10

PIT OF CAPTIVITY, OPPRESSION, AND ABJECT POVERTY

Every morning, while the morning dew was still on the grass, the guards paraded us into the black mud, up to our knees, or higher. One morning, more than the usual number of hungry leeches floated in the water. The mass of disgusting creatures scared me, especially when they wrapped around my ankles and sank their teeth into me. I never understood why they attached to me more than most of the others.

The pain and nervousness slowed me down until I had the courage to make myself pull them off. My fingers swept over my ankle and found one of the black, slimy, elastic creatures the size of my thumb stuck like glue to me.

For fear of being labeled "weak," I tried holding my breath to keep from screaming while pulling hard enough to remove it from me. Every time one lost its grip on me, with bits of my skin and my blood dripping from its mouth, I shuddered and cried out, partly with relief and partly due to the pain.

In my group, most people had been field workers, so their lives weren't much different than before. They were used to hard physical labor and spoke of being content with the Khmer Rouge's rule over us.

They laughed about my fear of the leeches and how I got behind in my work pulling them off. Some talked to the Khmer Rouge group leader about me and somehow found out my husband was a high-ranking military officer. They criticized the way I walked, bullied me for being married to someone from the previous government, and brought attention to every mistake that I made.

They called people like me by certain names, such as "Metoun," which meant "rich boss." By that time, I understood the communist regime targeted everyone who belonged to the middle class or wealthy families since they were most likely to resist their new socialist/communist government. Khmer Rouge systematically eliminated anyone with money or education. Only a few with any social standing still survived.

The leader of the Khmer Rouge woman's group hated everything I symbolized in society: educated and wealthy. At least I had been well off financially, before. Now, everyone sank into this pit of captivity, oppression, and abject poverty. One woman with gold front teeth and short hair, in a black uniform, seemed to take particular pleasure in glaring at me. I feared she was devising a torturous way to kill me herself.

I worked as hard as I could and tried to ignore the leeches sucking the little life remaining in me. While I worked, I fantasized that one day my husband might rescue me. I remembered our lavish lifestyle and estate. I imagined how we would soon go back to it, raising Alex, just the way we dreamed.

Then reality bit me on the ankle. I swiped at another blood-sucking leech and wondered how I would be able to keep my promise to provide for Alex. Were my brothers able to get help for us? Had they survived the minefields? Could Pa be out there somewhere, looking for us, if he survived?

I tossed a few strands of hair in front of my face. Much of my formerly thick hair had fallen out. What remained was dry and stringy, like the peasant women I used to pity. The brittle stray locks and the sweat disguised my tears from my coworkers and the soldiers.

My sisters were much younger than I. They, my mother, and my son had been taken to work in different zones far away from me. At least they still worked with Mom and could take care of Alex. I would see them again, one day.

The backbreaking work, isolation, constant criticism, and mocking took a toll mentally and physically. My hands and legs developed tremors. My brain struggled between the hope of rescue and the reality around me. How long could I survive living like this?

Living with no apparent hope of rescue seemed a better option than waking to dashed hopes every day. My mind protected me by blocking out what I left behind. I plodded through my assigned tasks, releasing my dreams of escape or rescue. For my sanity, I focused on survival, if you could call it that, from one dawn to the next.

* * *

One morning, instead of having me walk down to work in the field, the same soldier who tried to come to my hut several months ago who was frightened away by my brothers, took me away from the others. He guided me to the river and told me to get into the canoe tied by the edge. At the time, I was frightened and confused about that soldier.

I bent over, stepped into the boat, and looked at the field workers behind us. They all stood, looking at me with solemn faces. We all knew that people who were taken away by soldiers did not return. I supposed they felt sorry for me, knowing I was about to be killed. Of course, none of them could react openly or say anything in front of our guards.

Resigning myself to the reality that this would be my last day of life, I cooperated. No point in causing undue agony. I tried to look at the beauty of the river and listen to the birds. If these were my last moments on earth, I wanted to have a good look at the grandeur of it. I would always remember my son, my father, and my brothers.

I lowered my head and sobbed in silence.

Why had no one come?

Who would tell my husband?

Would someone in the family survive and tell Alex about me in the future, or would he forget me?

I wrapped my arms around my bony body, hoping to steady my trembling shoulders.

The guard rowed without speaking to me.

I didn't dare address him.

The sound of gunfire blasted in the trees. I crouched over for protection.

Some limbs hanging above the river bounced up and down as some birds took flight. Mynah birds. There was no gunfire, only the birds mimicking what they had heard.

I smiled at the thought of our family bird until I realized we didn't take him out of the cage. Perhaps one of the staff took him home or maybe he remained in the cage catching insects and vrooming in the carport.

The distraction helped settle my shoulders, but my heart palpitated with an unruly beat. I kept my hands in front of me, ready for the paddle to swing around and knock me out of consciousness to die in the water. If he didn't kill me in the boat, I hated to think of what would await me. My throat tightened and I remembered my father told me how much strength I would need.

Somehow, he knew.

Pa, I promised you I'd be strong. I would be strong and fearless like Mom. I would keep my promise to him, as long as I had breath in me.

Chapter 11

TAKEN AWAY—TO PARADISE

After several hours of only the sounds of the water and birds, it seemed to me that we were headed from the river into the ocean. I could only see water around us until we came to an island.

I had no idea what to expect there, other than supposing he singled me out to go to some sort of death camp or prostitution camp. Why else would he take me away from the others?

He pulled the canoe into a shallow place and told me to get out. People came and went without paying much attention to us. It didn't seem like a work camp, at least not like the one where I had been.

The people dressed casually and seemed happy to be going about their lives. If the Khmer Rouge were directing their every move, it didn't show in the way they behaved. They seemed to live in freedom.

It appeared that these people had lived there all their lives, that the Khmer Rouge had never bordered them. Perhaps it was the same place they originally came from. I saw only a few in the military black uniforms with red krama or scarves. Even after several minutes, I didn't see anyone wearing Khmer Rouge headbands.

The soldier pointed for me to come to the island with him. After we reached the cover of some trees within a village, he simply told me to stay there, and then he walked away from me and left.

Some villagers came and chatted with me. They mostly wore modern clothes. A middle-aged lady in a traditional sarong invited me to stay in a safe place next to a large, older building where she lived.

I settled in and watched the people. No one glared at me or gave me orders. They all went about their own business, fishing, cooking, and living. I flinched in fear when the first few people came to talk to me, expecting to be put into shackles or enslaved, but we just had a friendly conversation.

I nearly cried.

How long had it been without friends or pleasant conversation? I couldn't even remember.

I covered my mouth when I nearly laughed about it, so they wouldn't think I was laughing at them. No one back in the rice fields would believe the soldier didn't kill me, much less that he had taken me to a better place.

That night, the woman shared her fish and rice—real rice, not a few grains floating in dirty water. Having my first few bites of such tasty and substantial food in such a long time, I swallowed slowly and savored every morsel. I wished I could have brought my family here.

I found an egg and hid it in a pocket for my son, with the hope I could somehow find my way back to him.

I rubbed my old neck injury. The tension from the thoughts of my death landed there and flared up the muscle and nerve pain. Rolling my head gingerly to loosen the tightness, I realized for the first time in a long time, I didn't feel afraid.

Everyone seemed compassionate and welcoming to me. When they learned I didn't know how to fish, they didn't beat me or berate me. It didn't matter to them.

The day before, I had been slaving under the blistering sun, in leech-filled, muddy water. Now, hope had returned. I smiled at the thought of living in freedom again and finding a way to get back to my family.

We lived together on the island, without pressure to perform labor in rice fields. Everyone helped one another and shared what they had.

At night, I heard a tumultuous uproar coming from the river. The locals said it was the result of too many fish hatching. My beautiful Cambodia, where the rumduol blooms and the fish supply never ends. In college, we learned Cambodia had more fish than neighboring Thailand or Vietnam. Many Vietnamese people had and still have commercial fishing businesses in Cambodia.

The villagers explained that fish from far away, including Thailand and Vietnam, came to lay eggs under the protection of weeds growing around the island.

A few months later, while I helped fishermen and their families pull in the fishing netting, I felt a sharp sting. I think someone told me it was a fish fin. I quickly drifted into unconsciousness.

When I woke, my mom and son were looking at me. I was as surprised to see them as they were to see me. At first, I thought I must have been dreaming.

My sister Thyda said she had seen a body floating on the river and called everyone to look. People came to help her drag the person, me, to shore. Somehow, I had been unconscious from the poison on the fish fin and floated to them.

When I became more alert, we talked about the events of the past months. When Mom and I were alone for a few minutes, she told me of a vivid dream she had the night before the soldier took me away. In the dream, she had seen a man with a long white mustache holding some sort of can. She said that he came to rescue me.

I truly felt rescued on that island, yet my heart still yearned to be with my family. I remembered the egg and pulled it out of my pocket. It was still intact but rotten. The one thing I could have given my son had become garbage, but at least I could be with him.

While I held Alex, Mom told me that while I was away he had suffered from rectal prolapse. Because we lived with parasites and disease, diarrhea had become our normal. And with that, often the intestines are pushed out too far. I picked him up to look at his face again. No sign of pain or distress.

"Don't worry, Srey Na."

As always, Mom knew what to do. She patted my arm. A villager told Mom about an old Khmer remedy. Mom found a rusty nail and boiled it with the sap from green papaya. After it cooled, she gave him some to drink. "Didn't I, Piseth?"

Alex smiled to hear his grandmother call him this special term of endearment. He playfully clapped his hands together while she spoke.

"Now, he's much better."

"Mom. You've always taken care of us. I don't know what I would do without you." I tried to contain the emotions bubbling inside. "If they take me away again and I don't get to . . ." I smoothed Alex's hair and kissed the top of his head.

Mom grabbed my wrist. "You're here now. You're okay. We all are." She held her breath for a moment.

Memories of Pa, my husband, and my brothers welled up in my eyes.

"Today, Srey Na," she spoke with a calm, slow voice, "you are here. I am here. Your son is in your lap. He knows you are here with him. Your blood flows in him. Be strong for today. None of us knows what tomorrow will bring."

I nodded. "I will, Mom." I lifted his small hand to my lips and kissed it.

So much had happened while I was away, yet when I returned, much remained the same. I still had Mom and Alex. Tomorrow at sunrise, I would work again in the rice fields. I had done it before my time on the island, and I could do it again, for them.

The soldier didn't kill me. The poison from the fish fin didn't kill me. They didn't know who my sister saw floating in the river or if they were alive, yet, they pulled me from the water. I didn't understand how or why, but I knew these had to be miracles.

With God watching over me, I could survive.

Chapter 12

BACK TO THE RICE FIELDS—SEPARATED FROM MY FAMILY

The next morning, the Khmer Rouge leader sent me away from the fields where my mother and my son stayed. They didn't offer me an explanation, but I imagined they wanted to punish me for my absence by separating me from my family.

I was surprised to see that my sister Thyda seemed not to be happy about my return. I tried to remember that after the loss we endured, the starvation, and the constant fear of death from the Khmer Rouge, we all had changed.

To survive, many people submitted to the Khmer Rouge's attitude of having little consideration for life. They had forced us into labor and deprivation. If we showed signs of resistance or weakness, our conditions worsened. If we still didn't conform to their standards, we died.

They gave so little value to our lives that we forgot how precious our lives and our families could be. Because they provided only enough rations to barely stave off death, we only thought of our survival from moment to moment. Our lives depended on the government and they made certain we all remembered it. They promoted hatred among us causing distrust, again so we would come to them, instead of to family or God. Our total submission appeared to be the goal, and they had excelled in techniques to achieve it.

A diet of ongoing hatred did awful things to people. After months of brainwashing about the evil of those who had been wealthy, Thyda seemed scared of me. She might have been afraid that soldiers would take me away again and take her with us. I didn't know what to do, so I stayed away from her when I could. My youngest sister also distanced herself from me.

The other workers also distanced themselves from me. None of them talked with me. I'm sure they all thought that if they became close to me, their lives would be in danger. I had been taken before and returned, how could they trust me? If the Khmer Rouge didn't kill me, I could have been sent back to spy on them. Or, I could still be targeted by being married to someone so wealthy.

I tried to understand, but the isolation added so much weight to my already dire situation.

* * *

Several months later, the rice was ready for harvest. The grain heads had ripened, turning from green to orangish-red. As the sun set, while walking back toward my shack, I watched the beautiful lush fields rise up and down with the motion of the air, like ocean waves undulating in the wind along a tiny sidewalk.

I remembered our rice fields and how I had loved to play there. The beauty of these fields brought an unexpected peace to my soul. Fear and hatred might have clouded everyone else, but God's nature refreshed my soul with calmness. The air seemed lighter with His goodness. The birds called out while they swooped to catch the rice moths. I felt as if He spoke to me, giving me the priceless gift of hope and joy with these fields that seemed to smile at me.

Late one evening after work, while I plodded from the fields in my muddy pants back to my shack, I caught a whiff of freshly cooked jasmine rice. That ignited an intense craving for it.

Even though the trail toward my shack had spectacular golden, ripe rice grains ready to harvest anytime, my daily rations of mostly water and fish bones included only a few grains of rice.

My hunger sparked an idea. A risky idea, but with no moon that night, I might be able to get away with it.

After everyone had gone to sleep, I returned to the rice field next to my shack to get some grains of rice. The darkness and quiet assured me that no one could see me. Crickets and frogs sang their nighttime songs and I put my plan into action.

I covered my head and face with a scarf and bent over in the lowest profile possible, making tiny quiet steps toward the rice field only a few steps from my shack. Stopping in the rice bushes, I looked around. Only the night insects chirped around me.

Hunkered down among the rice bushes, I gently pulled several handfuls of rice from the stem and wrapped them in my scarf. My weakened hands fumbled a good many of the precious grain heads. I quietly scooped up as many as I could. I didn't dare take too much time and risk being caught. Thank God, I got away with it this time.

Back in the shack, I stashed the rice in some clothing before I lay down to sleep. "Thank you, God, for protecting me and allowing me to have this extra food." I never dreamed I would be so thankful to slosh in the mud for a few heads of rice.

That night, I dreamed of removing the husks and cooking the fragrant rice. In my dream, my mother and son were with me devouring the wonderful treat.

I woke to reality. Mom and Alex were back at the main camp. I was still at a remote location. I patted beside me for the rice, smiling when my hands found the long strands. I would find the time to remove the husk and add it to my ration that night if I could.

During the day, I thought of the hidden rice. It gave me strength just knowing I would soon be able to enjoy it. I lightly shook the heads and a few grains fell out into the fabric. I secretly prepared the rice and ate it alone. If I had added it to my gruel and fish soup, everyone would have known I had stolen it, so I ate it away from everyone else. I closed my eyes and savored the substance and flavor. Slave camp food suddenly had a glimmer of hope.

* * *

I continued to eat gruel and fish soup, like everyone else, for many months until the second year of living in the deadly zone, when another wave of near starvation hit us.

While we cut and tied bundles of rice, I noticed some workers hid rice in their pants and rolled their sleeves up to hide a little more.

I was nervous to take the chance in the daylight but saw so many doing it, that I didn't want to miss an opportunity.

They had made a pocket in their pants by having a strong string to tie a knot at the bottom of their pants legs. I looked for something to tie my pants at the last minute; all I found was several long pieces of rice straw lying on the ground next to me. I knew those pieces of straw weren't as strong as the string, but I had no other choice, so I went ahead and tied several pieces around my pants at my ankles and hoped it would be strong enough to last until I reached my shack.

We all knew that soldiers killed workers for less than stealing a few heads of rice, but months of malnutrition emboldened us to take the risk.

I slid in more and more rice as I made my way down the rows. My pants became heavy and bulged noticeably. When we finished working, and I stepped onto dry land, the heavy mud and water flushed down my pants. The straw knot broke, more easily than I expected, causing all my hidden grain to drop down out of my pants and onto the dry ground in front of everyone. How stupid I was.

A soldier and the group leader saw the stolen rice spill from my pants leg. All the other workers watched in silence for a moment while I shook in fear with the soldier screaming at me. They scurried away to the safety of their shacks while all attention was on me. How could I have been so stupid?

As I expected, that evening just before sunset, I was taken away from everyone else and left alone with a few soldiers. The next day, while everyone else was back working in the field, I was taken to meet several soldiers and top leaders whom I had never seen before. I stood surrounded by them while they talked to one another. Among them was the soldier who had taken me away by canoe. He was staring at me, saying nothing. My disobedience deserved death according to the Khmer Rouge's Angkar law.

Chapter 13

MIRACLES HAPPEN

Suddenly, a good-looking, tall, and skinny young soldier, whom I had never seen before, made his way to the front of everyone there. He stood at attention and asserted, "I ask everyone's permission to take this girl with me. I will kill her with my own hands."

From his demeanor and stance, I had little doubt he meant what he said.

The leaders agreed and this man took me with him. We rode on a horse, away from the group.

After we were away from any place I recognized, he pulled me off the horse. I knew I didn't have the strength to fight off a young soldier and fully expected to draw my last breath at his hand, as he had promised. I thought of Alex, my husband, Mom, and Pa while I waited for my execution, but instead, I heard the horse gallop away. I turned around, and the soldier/executioner rode off on the horse.

Stunned, I watched him go down the path still bearing the hoofprints from moments before. After a moment, he disappeared.

I was alive.

He didn't harm me. I must be dreaming.

I heard rustling around me and saw some villagers I didn't recognize coming to greet me. I didn't know where I was, and I certainly didn't know how I was still alive.

This group of people was younger, more friendly than those I worked with at the camp; this place seemed like an older, established small village. They were cordial and must have been the original villagers. I think many members of the Khmer Rouge were originally from the countryside; they were safer than those who came from the city. This group of people must have been established there before the war, because their houses were made of much taller and stronger building materials, instead of bamboo or straw.

Another miracle. God had spared my life a second time. I wondered if miracles occur when we are out of our comfort zone. I was not only outside my comfort zone, I was lost.

This community wove fabric with a loom and used the material to make clothing. With smiling faces, they invited me to join them.

I couldn't help thinking how wonderful to live and work among such happy people. I also enjoyed this type of work. The environment was much better. Instead of being in constant fear, everyone was friendly. They shared their food and fresh fruits with me.

How I wished I could see Mom and Alex and share this with them. While thankful to be in better conditions, I sorely missed my family.

With survival my goal, my brain didn't provide me with the memory of how long I was there or how I returned to meet my son and my mother, again. I have no idea how I knew the route from there back to the field where I worked but I did return.

As you can imagine, my return from being taken for execution did not sit well with the group leaders and others who hated me. They warned me that I would be under close supervision.

Atrocious rumors about me annoyed the entire village, and word of them reached the group leaders. They and the soldiers decided to remove me from everyone and brought me under their direct supervision. Here I was surrounded by mostly women Khmer Rouge group leaders who were prone to murder anyone without a shred of evidence.

I gave up the hope of joining my son and my mother again. The workers all feared being near me this time. I was the only one from the city. The Khmer Rouge leaders had a great time celebrating among themselves while preparing to kill me.

Among the group leaders, I recognized one woman with a gold front tooth—my original group leader. This very dangerous and nasty woman had always stared at me with evil intentions in her eyes. She took great joy in expressing how excited she was to kill me once and for all.

There was no reason for her animosity toward me, much less the venomous outbursts. Every few minutes she derided me with a reminder of how she looked forward to seeing me die.

That evening, everyone was enjoying poking fun at and mocking me. They added the accusation of me being married to a powerful political leader whom the Khmer Rouge hated the most. Of course, that made them hate me even more.

Later that night, my captors had me sleep in their building with them, surrounded by tight security. We all slept on the hardwood floor side by side. The whole floor was filled with people and I had no space to move.

I fell asleep for a couple of hours and woke up with a strong urge to urinate. I couldn't wait for sunrise, so I chose to go outside. I had to carefully crawl around people, careful not to disturb anyone. I couldn't see in the darkness, so I used my arm to try and navigate my way out.

I had held in the urge so long, it was about to leak out whether I made it outside or not. My arm touched something that felt like a bowl. I took advantage of the opportunity and tried to keep it from getting on anyone. As soon as I finished, I placed the bowl on the floor and crawled back to my spot, desperately hoping no one would wake up.

The next morning, someone found their bowl had urine in it. One person said something, and suddenly shouting erupted all around me. They became furious, realizing that I was the one who had peed in it.

"Take her to kill! Take her to kill!" they yelled. Everyone in the building joined the frenzy and screamed and pointed at me.

In shock, I fell unconscious.

When I regained consciousness, I was in a building with a long and rectangular shape. Through the slits in the wall, I could see vast fields around me. It felt like an isolated, secret prison camp, built with bamboo with a straw rooftop. I saw only two soldiers who took turns guarding me.

Later, I overheard the soldiers talking with one another, saying that when I fell unconscious, they were debating whether they should hang me by my ankles from a tree and let the birds eat me or whether they should bring me to the prison camp to let the prosecutor murder me the same way they kill other prisoners.

I wasn't sure where I was or how I got there. My brain felt numb, and my body shook, knowing that I would never be able to see my son and my mother again. I couldn't shake the feeling that sooner or later I would be killed. In the meantime, I waited alone. I stared through the slits at the clear blue sky. The full sun bore down on the building without shade. For days, I sat.

Waiting.

Alone.

One afternoon, a soldier opened the door and ordered me to follow him. At least that took me out of the bamboo box and into the fresh air. I was out of isolation and looked at the cloudless sky and felt a slight breeze against my face. I walked behind him for several hours, until we reached an area that was wooded on one side.

The place had an eerie, foreboding feel. I sighed. God, if You have any more miracles left for me, this would be a good time for one.

Then, a shield of clouds or smoke, as white as a sheet of cotton swirling in the air, formed above our heads and descended toward us. I turned around, looking for someone who could rescue me, who might be burning something, but I didn't see anyone. There was no smell, no smoke, no flame, no fire of any kind. It was deathly quiet; all I could see was a vast open field on one side and a dense forest on the other. What a frightening place to be.

Cambodia is not known for dense clouds or fog. This was something very extraordinary.

My breathing quickened.

I looked for an escape route.

What was happening? The sky had been clear just minutes before, with no storm clouds or thunder around us. Even so, this massive cloud encompassed us and grew so thick that I could no longer see the soldier who stood only a few feet from me. I only saw the whiteness of the cloud, nothing else.

The fog engulfed us. I couldn't hear the breeze in the tree limbs, birds, or anything. I felt like I had been immersed underwater in this dense cloud, leaving me claustrophobic and disoriented. I reached out to feel my way out of it and tried to restrain the panic that welled in me.

When the fog cleared, and I could hear the normal outdoor sounds again, I looked around for the soldier. He was nowhere to be found. I turned around several times, looking for any sign of him.

Free again, I thought of how to get back to Mom and Alex. Judging by the sun, it must have been around four or five in the late afternoon. Unsure of my exact location, I recognized I was still in a large field heavily wooded on one side.

God must have provided one more miracle for me.

Which way would I travel to get back to my mother and son?

Thinking back, all those years, I was so confused, so blinded, and never fully realized that God existed, but something was always telling me that there was a God who was protecting me, whether or not I knew who God was. What I did know was that if He provided that miracle, then I needed to trust Him to guide me to my family.

I started walking with no idea of which direction to travel, so I followed the sun. My body felt noticeably light and I kept moving.

Exhausted but refreshed with a spark of hope, I traveled alone from one place to another. I got lost in a vast field with only the birds and insects to keep me company. From the rice field that seemed as big as the ocean, I watched the sun sink closer to the horizon.

As the vibrant greens around me and everything transformed into shades of gray, I believed that God was there with me. He had intervened. He had seen everything and had protected me from being killed these three different times.

I walked alone in the dusk. My mind and body were both so weary I could barely function. Strange things, perhaps hallucinations, appeared. Monsters. Some dressed colorfully, and some bore ugly faces. They jeered at me in a language I couldn't understand. Even in my debilitating fatigue, I was terrified, my heart was pounding so fast that all I could think of was to run as fast as I could, hoping to reach the village where I could get closer to people.

I don't know how long I walked, but late that night, I somehow found my way to the village where my son and mother were staying. With everyone asleep, a deep quiet covered the camp. I found the shack where I last saw Alex and Mom and went in.

By the light of a small lantern she had burning, I saw Mom, still awake and sitting by herself. Without a word to alert anyone, she motioned for me to come and sleep beside her. I laid down with my head in her lap. I had thought I would never again see her, much less sleep under the same roof with my precious mom.

She massaged the place where the soldier had hit my neck long ago. I wept in the joy and relief of the moment and drifted into a blissful sleep in Mom's embrace. If this were a dream, I wanted to stay asleep for a long time.

Chapter 14

MOTHER DIES, BUT WE ARE SET FREE

When we got up the next morning, I heard people whispering, "Look at her. She's practically a walking corpse. How did she get away and come back a third time?"

Considering how I felt, I wasn't surprised to hear how I looked.

I had recognized her voice in the darkness, but in the light of day, I was alarmed to see how skinny my mother had become. Her features were unrecognizable. She had become frail and had lost a lot of weight, even beyond the starvation conditions.

She worked next to a tobacco field and had fed her hunger with cigarettes, one after another.

She left her beautiful home, the plantations, with only a few belongings. Her husband had been taken from us, her two older loving sons were gone with no hope of return, and her other three teenagers were also taken away. She had watched me be taken away to be killed several times. My heart ached to see her strong spirit so broken. This remarkable woman had built and lost so much and yet kept going the best she could while everything collapsed around her.

That same year was the first time the guards sent Thyda to work at a different camp not far away from me and away from Mom and Alex. I didn't know until that night that we were to sleep on the ground by a campfire. Later that night, I felt a bug crawl into my ear. It had to have been small to get in my ear canal, but it felt huge. The pressure made it seem like an elephant was trying to make a home there. I struggled to get it out and relieve the pressure, but it only tried to go deeper.

While I struggled to corral the insect, on the other side of the campfire, I heard Thyda's voice, talking and laughing and having a great time together with several women from her group. I heard them talking about having marijuana in their food. When I looked past her, through the burning flame, I could see several full-grown marijuana bushes next to them. They ignored my distress and continued their conversation about how marijuana made them feel so happy.

Still captive to the brainwashing of the Khmer Rouge, Thyda often belittled me as the wife of a high-ranking official. To the Khmer Rouge, everyone of wealth or political power was an enemy. They had heard the propaganda for so long, they believed it. Even now, my sisters joke that the ground "refused to bury me." From that point, Thyda no longer acted like my younger sister. She turned her back on me and would find reasons to fight with me any time she saw me.

Three years later, they took me back to the camp where Mom and Alex were. Mom wanted to erase the previous narrative about me and changed my name from Peou Kuna (nicknamed Srey Na) to simply Pheap, meaning "peace." I now feel as though God had given me a new name.

She told me, "Tell anyone who asks who you are, you are Pheap. You have cheated death three times and are now to be called Pheap. Never again mention your former name."

With this new identity, I could have a fresh start apart from my privileged past and establish a new identity. Because I had been gone a long time from this camp and now used a different name, no one bullied me or recognized me as they had before. My wise mother gave me many precious gifts, and this was one of them.

* * *

Not long after I returned to the camp with Mom and Alex, our guards and group leaders decided to let us go one day, and we didn't argue. Looking back, I wonder if the military leaders recognized me after all and realized they had failed to kill me. Perhaps they didn't want us around as a reminder.

Our family—my mother, two sisters, my son, and I—were the only ones ordered to move from our shack and out of the work camp. With that clear order, we didn't ask for an explanation. We set out barefoot but free.

Thyda asked Mom to leave me behind so I would go my own way instead of traveling with the rest of the family. Mom ignored her and we headed out together, hoping to find a safe place to stay.

Mom had always been a strong and resilient woman. When she told me she felt that something was not right with her, I knew it had to be bad. She had become so weak that she could hardly walk anymore. I didn't notice it so much in the camp, but on the road, she struggled to keep up.

"Pheap." She whispered to me, "I don't know if I can make it."

I stopped and looked at her pale and gaunt face. Her cloudy eyes darted, but she didn't seem to be able to focus. I steadied her arm and walked beside her.

What if she was right and couldn't make it?

No.

I refused to consider it. When tears brimmed my eyelids, I blinked them back. I couldn't afford any negative thoughts to steal the little energy I had left. I reminded myself we were finally reunited, but my heart was so broken to see Mom in this condition. I was scared to say anything, though, knowing that my sisters weren't happy about having me around. We lived through the most harrowing of times and now we could begin a new life together, as a family, but we were no longer the same. I had to be strong to encourage Mom and my son to keep going. We had all drawn from her unwavering strength in the face of adversity. She held our family together.

We walked in the scorching heat to the point of exhaustion each day. With no trees or even bushes to provide a cool place to rest, we continued in the dry heat. Occasionally, we flicked the salty crust from our faces, so we didn't accidentally scratch it across our already sunburned skin. As the sun lowered in the west, I looked behind us and saw that we had navigated over sandy hills. I felt some relief that we could no longer see the work village or rice fields, yet we had no place to go, either.

By the time darkness had set in, we had reached a village. Mom had pushed her body as far as she could to stay with us. But, when we sat down, her breathing became labored. We were exhausted. We knew no one we could ask for help and, instead, watched her through the night.

At dawn, some people in the village came to look at Mom. One of them—probably a Khmer Rouge leader—requested to send her away to be treated. We knew she needed help and agreed to let her go. Thyda and Alex went with her. They had lived together for over three years in the deadly zone without me and were incredibly close.

I had forgotten about it, but Mom still had the pouch of my jewelry I had left with her the first time I was taken from the work camp. I was reminded of it when Thyda tried to return it to me, but I insisted that she use it to help pay for Mom's medical treatment.

A few days later, Thyda returned with the pouch but without Mom. I had thought my jewelry would help to pay for Mom's medical treatment. She was sick and needed it. Why would Thyda return it to me? Then, an unforgettable sinking feeling in my heart told me that something had gone wrong with Mom.

A wave of the unthinkable washed over me. I mouthed to Mom, as if she were standing beside me, "I love you, Mom. I love you, so much." I wanted to see her, but I was not allowed.

Thyda told me Mom had passed away. Grief filled every pore of my body and I convulsed in uncontrollable heartache. Tears streamed down my face from some of the deepest and most unforgettable emotional pain that I've ever felt. I thought I must have been dying too.

When I could breathe again, I took some solace knowing she lived her last days in freedom. How could I live without my parents? My husband? My brothers? And what of my son who was always by her side?

I shuddered and wept until exhaustion didn't allow any more.

Alex had lived with Mom the last few years while I had been sent away. From the time he opened his eyes till the time he fell asleep, he cried for her. In many ways, it was as if his mom had died too.

When we buried my mother, he pointed his small hands toward her grave and sobbed, "Mama. Mama. Mama." My little boy's body shook badly, and he cried so loudly it took my breath away.

Seeing him so heartbroken magnified my sorrow. I wondered how my heart had the strength to keep beating in this agonizing moment.

I was so thankful that both of my sisters helped take care of Alex while I mourned. Just when hope had surfaced, this loss pulled me into an unending pit of sorrow. I wondered if I had the physical and mental stamina to carry on.

After three and a half years of hatred and propaganda within the work camps and living under the continual threat of death, I doubted my ability to think. Maybe even to live.

I knew life would never be the same again for any of us. This was especially true for my son. Before we had been separated, he had reached for me and clung to me as his mom. Now, I was practically a stranger to him. Who was I now, if not a big sister, a daughter, a wife, or a mom?

I had no idea if my husband was still alive. My sisters no longer treated me as a sister. With the loss of my parents and my brothers, I felt that no one wanted me or cared for me. Still, I desperately wanted to take care of my son, but I was depleted in mind, spirit, and body.

1979

About a week after Mom died, Vietnamese military trucks stormed into the area. We heard multiple rounds of gunshots. Shortly after, the fleeing Khmer Rouge soldiers' feet stirred up dust on the roads. We recognized the Vietnamese soldiers because they didn't wear the black Khmer Rouge uniforms with a red krama around their neck, and they wore black rubber sandals instead of real boots. They wore real uniforms and announced Pol Pot had been overthrown and that we now lived in the People's Republic of Kampuchea.

Some of them carried guns, but only to remove the Khmer Rouge soldiers. They told us we were free and carried medical supplies. When I saw the Vietnamese troops and the medical supplies they were carrying, I wished I could bring my mother back from her grave to give her treatment that could have saved her life.

I wanted to yell at them for not coming earlier. If it would have changed anything, I would have screamed at the top of my lungs. But the days when we could have helped her had passed. I was powerless to bring her back or change the passing of time.

Because we were in the northernmost part of the country, we didn't realize the Vietnamese People's Republic of

Kampuchea had taken over the Khmer Rouge regime. I knew from history, that the borders between Vietnam and Cambodia had fluctuated through the years. In the 1600s, a Khmer king married a Vietnamese woman and the two countries flourished together, especially along the Mekong delta. During that time, Cambodia controlled the area of Prey Nokor, later called Saigon, and known as Ho Chi Minh City after the Vietnamese took over.

Now, the Vietnamese had come to rescue us from communism. They started in the south part of Cambodia, and village by village, they finally reached us. The Khmer Rouge military fled toward the Thai border, village by village, making their way north. Without any outside news since 1975, we had no idea of the political situation. We only knew what the Khmer Rouge told us.

Under the new government, we were again free to go anywhere we wanted. Our newfound freedom made the air seem fresher and the sun shine brighter. I had taken so much for granted before the evacuation. Once we were treated with basic human kindness again, I realized how much dignity the Khmer Rouge had taken from us.

A day with freedom is a gift I will never again take for granted.

Chapter 15

LOVED ONES FOUND AND LOVED ONES LEFT

We were overjoyed to have the Vietnamese soldiers intervene in this Cambodian holocaust. We embraced being treated like human beings again.

With freedom to speak, move, and find our own way, people searched for their loved ones. My brother Rick found us.

When I had last seen him nearly four years ago, he and our two younger brothers had been taken to work away from the rest of us. Now he stood before me, as an eighteen-year-old young man. He had grown into a strong young man.

I could see Pa in his features, and tears filled my eyes again for my beloved father. I told Rick the heartbreaking news about the brothers who left the killing fields.

He looked around. "What about Mom?"

When I told him, he put his hands to his pained face and shook his head. "Srey Na, if I had only been able to come earlier and see Mom and our brothers again."

I nodded. "That would have been so good for her—for us all."

While we were all happy to have my brother join us, we still mourned the recent death of Mom. The anguish probably fell heavier on Alex than on the rest of us. He often cried for his grandma. He became so grief-stricken, he refused to eat.

Even after all I had endured, watching his grief brought me to a breaking point. I fell into a deep pit of despair, wishing I had died along with my mother.

I had been so focused on survival for the last four years, I suppose I didn't give myself room to grieve. Now that the threat of immediate death didn't hover over us in red scarves, the reality of moving forward without my husband, my father, my mother, and three brothers hit me hard. My heart ached in excruciating pain, sorrow, and emptiness.

Rick reasoned out a plan of action. "We don't know where Pa is. Even though Ma is buried here, we need to leave. I have a horse-drawn wagon. Pack up whatever you have and come with me to Battambang."

I looked toward Mom's grave and hesitated.

He held my shoulders and turned me to face him. "Srey Na. We can't change the past. We are together now. Let's move forward. That's what Pa and Mom would want."

He was right. We had no way to bring the dead back to life. Mom put one foot in front of the other as long as she could. I could do the same. I promised Pa I would. We were family and would get through this together. I was still the oldest sister and I had responsibilities to them.

The hatred that had poisoned Thyda surfaced again. While we packed the wagon, I heard her ask Rick to leave me behind and to kick me out of the family. I tried to understand her state of mind. We had all suffered torture both physically and mentally.

Rick ignored her, and we left the jungle village aboard his wagon, headed for Battambang, a city in northwestern Cambodia on the edge of the Sangkae River. His girlfriend lived there. He had also found our younger brothers, Notch and David.

I found another reason to be thankful—at least part of the family had survived.

Our younger brother David told me about when they took him away from us. He had been given the job of digging trenches and canals on the front lines, allowing the water to flow into the rice fields. My heart lightened to hear his voice. I gained strength from being with my brothers again. Our family bond healed some of my innermost wounds. Ma would have been so happy to see us together again.

* * *

In the short time we stayed in Battambang, I grew to love the crowded marketplace. Seeing people live in freedom, buying and selling goods, and speaking freely reminded me of life before the war. After living in desolate conditions, it felt so good to be around people again.

I met several people there who had stayed in the same zone with us in the killing fields. At the market, when I passed by them, they were astonished to see me alive and well. Some spoke to me. Others spoke in hushed tones with their fingers to their lips while looking at me.

Now and then I heard a few of their words: "Is she still alive and safe?"

"Is that her? I thought she was dead."

Some of them rubbed their eyes when they saw me, asking, "Is that you? Didn't the Khmer Rouge take you away to be killed several times?"

I took pleasure in assuring them I was not dead, contrary to reports otherwise. Their confusion was understandable. I always found it funny I had to convince people who knew the Khmer Rouge had taken me away for execution more than once, and yet I remained alive.

* * *

As our new lives in freedom set in, I remembered my parents and all their hard work. I thought of our days at the plantation, rice fields, and our home. They had labored so long to give us good lives and provide income for future generations.

Bitterness took hold within me knowing the communist Khmer Rouge had stripped all our family land and wealth. They told us it was for the common good and it would bring equality to all the people. Somehow, they told us it was unfair that some people had earned wealth and possessions. Maybe it was just their propaganda to bring the poor on their side. They villainized everyone who had businesses and money, making me and my parents enemies in their society.

My parents' dreams and lives had been extinguished for no reason, other than the communist hatred for anyone who had education or money and who didn't submit to their control.

I wept for many days over the injustice. I didn't understand how so many people worked in the Khmer Rouge regime to force us to submit to it. How could they have killed so many innocent people whose only "crime" had been to earn a living? Why did my husband have to die? Why did they take Pa?

I cried to God for redemption and vindication. Our parents' properties were taken over by strangers. Whoever got their hands on the property before the owners returned occupied and remodeled. These strangers had taken possession of everything we had along with our futures. They now lived in the luxury Pa and Mom had worked for, in properties and businesses they didn't earn. They took our dreams. Our plans. All the money, time, and hard work we invested. They took it all and no one was being held accountable for it.

Though all my remaining family lived together with Rick and his girlfriend, we had been through so much physical and mental anguish that we never resumed our family dynamic as it had been before the war.

Instead of being thankful to be alive and together, my sister Thyda still talked of me as if I were the enemy. I had reasoned that the communist propaganda poisoned the soldiers, but coming from my sister, those accusations opened wounds my mind couldn't sort out. The echoes of hatred I had heard over the last years along with the injustice, frustration, and anger within me clouded my thoughts. I had lived in a survival mode for years, and now a fight-or-flight response took over me.

I had no strength to fight and no desire to fight with my sister. In that state of mind, I only knew I had to escape.

Although I had nowhere to go, I had to leave and was willing to sleep on the streets to get away. I didn't want that for Alex. He deserved better.

I made the irrational choice to leave alone and topped it off with another bad decision. I didn't tell anyone goodbye or even that I was leaving. Walking out that day, I relinquished my place as a big sister to my siblings and as a mother to my son.

Perhaps a doctor might have called it a nervous breakdown, but I only knew I had to get away. I had no idea where to go or of anyone to whom I could turn for help, but I walked out the door, leaving what was left of my family behind.

I wandered on the streets from one place to another, without any destination in mind. The tears I had withheld for the last years could no longer be restrained and streamed down my face and neck. My heart ached over being separated from my son again. I wept because I didn't know whom to trust. I cried because my heart could no longer hold in all the anguish from what I had endured.

Rick and his girlfriend had been so sweet. While I had been falling apart, Rick had done everything he could to keep us all together. He kept everyone alive through that time, providing food, lodging, and a family relationship for each of us. Rick was the hero who rescued us, and I never got the chance to express my gratitude to him.

I regretted leaving them without any explanation. As I got away from the house, I felt the pouch on my waistband that held my remaining jewelry. I had worn it for so long, I didn't remember it was there. I should have given it to them.

Why hadn't I retained the strength as the eldest sister to take the lead and help with the younger ones? If I had found the strength, I would have tried to recover our home and properties. It had fallen to me to protect their fortune, and I didn't.

I had no more strength or hope. My failures and regrets haunted me as I wandered the streets, useless to anyone, waiting to die.

Chapter 16

SOUL ENTERS MY LIFE

A lifeless skeleton, I headed in no particular direction. I heard survivors share stories of their losses and learned my husband had been killed shortly after he left us. The Khmer Rouge stormed our home and killed him. If Alex and I had been there, we would have been among the dead that day.

One day, while I was sitting alone in tears, someone called out, my name. "Kuna. Kuna?"

When I turned toward the sound of the voice, I saw a young man.

He asked, "Do you remember me?"

I scanned his face and build. My scrambled brain couldn't identify him. "No." I shook my head. "I'm sorry." I raised my shoulders. "I don't remember you."

"I'm Soul." He patted his chest. "Don't you remember me? I used to sit behind you in class when we were in college in Tuol Kork Phnom Penh. Remember?"

I sifted through my memories.

He tried to help me remember. "We attended Baccalaureate Part I and Part II before I was accepted into the University of Medicine in Phnom Penh, before the war." He leaned toward me with a hopeful look on his face.

I wiped my tearstained cheeks while I tried to think. I couldn't recall having any contact with male friends in my class. I never expected anyone from my class to be living in Battambang. It was nice to see a smiling face. I returned his smile.

He looked incredibly happy and handsome. We talked about college and the memories we had in common. It lifted a heavy burden within me to chat with someone who wanted to be my friend.

Because I was alone, I asked him if he would help me. Without going into details of how I ended up alone, I told him that I needed a place to stay and that I needed a job.

He told me that he could help. Soul's father was a physician in charge of Battambang Hospital. He had been a doctor there for several years before the war and remained a respectable, well-known doctor in town. Soul said, "I'll ask my father if you can work with him."

We talked about the time since we had been apart. I had married during the time he was in medical school. He had known my deceased brothers, and he also knew my parents very well.

He took me back to Battambang, to the hospital. Soul introduced me to every member who worked there and mentioned my father's name. Everyone recognized my father's name and welcomed me.

That acceptance and working alongside these friendly people breathed fresh air into my life. For the first couple of nights, I worked and trained at the hospital. A week later, Soul took me to his parents' house and asked his mother to let me stay with them. She agreed.

It had been a long time since anyone had shown me such kindness. I had held on to hope through the war for some sign of life from my husband. I listened for a sense of his spirit calling to me to wait for him.

I accepted that he had died. Gradually, I prayed for a fresh start. I could no longer carry the immense burden of the losses I had suffered. My time with Soul lightened the heaviness of my soul, including the resentment I had felt from some family members.

After the long days I spent working at the hospital, I would go to Soul's parents' house and help their maid cook and clean. The days were quite long, but I wanted to keep myself busy. With this safe place to live and a job, perhaps one day my son could join me. We could have a life together after all.

I didn't realize that Soul's parents had already set up an arranged marriage for him with their friend's daughter, a common practice among the upper class. They wanted Soul, their eldest son, to marry someone who would be close with their friends.

However, Soul now spent his time off with me. We did everything together. After a while, he told his parents he refused to marry the girl they had chosen.

I came home one evening after working at the hospital and heard a young child crying loudly. I looked in and saw

Alex by himself at the ground-level entrance to Soul's parents' house. He sat alone with no one to comfort him. He was wide-eyed and sobbing, screaming so loud for help. I wasn't sure how long Soul's mother had left my little boy crying alone. Shattered to see him in such distress, I lifted him in my arms and held him. "Alex, my precious son. I'm here. I love you. You're okay now." I was so angry at Soul's mother that my whole body shook.

Later that evening, when Soul came home, I told him what had happened. Soul, Alex, and I went to meet Thyda. She told me she had found out where I lived and dropped off my son there.

When Soul's mother found out about my situation, she turned her back on my son and left him to cry alone. Wealthy families not only arranged proper marriages for their children but also refused to consider a widow with a child a suitable mate.

I'm sure Soul's mother felt sorrow over not having the daughter-in-law she had chosen, but I didn't understand why she allowed my son to suffer alone, waiting for me to come home. I had the feeling she thought it would hurt me as much as my presence had hurt her plans for her son.

Soul and I had no place of our own, so we returned to live with his parents. I only had Alex and Soul and I would do whatever I could to hold on to them and our hopes for a future together.

His parents became cold toward me. I understood from their actions and words that they would never accept Alex or me. One day, when I came home, Soul had left. I didn't know where he might be or if I would ever hear from him again. While I waited to hear from him, I worked, took care of Alex, and tried to smile through my fears of another loss. We had such joy together; now all our dreams had floated out of reach.

After weeks of not hearing from Soul, I received a letter from him. At least I knew he was alive. I carefully tore open the envelope.

"Dear Kuna, my parents gave me money to fly to Australia, but instead, I went to Thailand. I'm in a refugee camp here and want you to join me. I already paid someone to walk you through the border to the camp. It's dangerous to come through the border at night, so don't bring Alex. We'll get settled here and send for him when we can."

Until I met Soul, my heart had found no reason to keep living. With Soul by my side, new strength came to me along with the will to move forward. I had to get to him and see if we could make a life together. So, I made arrangements for my son to stay with my brothers and sisters while I went to Thailand.

I reasoned that it would be to my son's benefit if all went as I hoped. Then, Soul, Alex, and I could live together and Alex would have a family again. I told myself that even though I had left him crying again, I would return to him soon and we would be together again forever.

While it hurt to leave him, I took comfort in knowing that if I encountered something bad on the journey to the border camp, I would be the one hurt. He would be safe.

I followed the instructions Soul had given me, and late that evening I met the guide who would take me to the border.

We walked in the darkness, deep inside the silent woods. I had no idea where we were.

Fear niggled at me. Every night call from an owl or rustle of the underbrush near us brought us to a halt. I held my breath and looked for thieves or red-scarved soldiers hiding, waiting to ambush us.

The steady sounds of insects in the otherwise quiet among the trees refreshed memories of nights in the shack by the rice fields. The snakes. Leeches. The bug in my ear. Hunger-filled nights with only evil surrounding me.

I shivered in the darkness. I'm in this wilderness with a man I don't know. I must trust him, but if something happened to him . . .

I couldn't let those thoughts take hold. I forced my brain to concentrate on being quiet and following his every footstep. While we tiptoed through a jungle of trees and undergrowth, my neck tightened. I tilted my head from side to side to release the tension. The blunt force neck injury from the butt of the soldier's rifle always flared up under stress. I forced my lungs to inhale and exhale as quietly as I could, concentrating on finding Soul and reuniting with Alex.

By daylight, we reached the refugee camp. As he promised, Soul waited for me there. The sight of him gave me a welcome burst of relief. I breathed fully again and smiled. I made it. We talked about how we could start our lives together. My protector, Soul, never left my side.

Chapter 17

UNICEF, RED CROSS—MONY BORN

Once again, our plans changed, this time because of the Thai government. They had no more resources for refugees and told us we had to go back to Cambodia. They loaded us into trucks and drove us to someplace near the jungle where they forced us to get out.

From there, we walked through very deep valleys. We trekked up and down hills along the Thai and Cambodian border for several weeks. Occasionally we found some food and water. It was good to be with Soul, at least.

I was thankful my son didn't have to suffer through this with us. He already had enough suffering in his life. With no place to go, and dying of starvation a growing possibility, we decided to return to the Thai refugee camp.

Though I never planned to leave my home country of Cambodia, my prayer for a fresh start seemed to point me to Thailand.

The Thai people gave me a new name, Virapheap Peou, meaning "victory." With my education and medical background, I found work at the Red Cross. For a couple of years, I worked there and later worked as a translator for UNICEF. They gave me a position at a German hospital. Soul did not have a job at the time, so he usually took care of errands at home.

At the hospital, I met a German doctor named Dr. Oskar Gartner. He asked questions about me and my family and we became friends. After a while, he told me he was in love with me and suggested that I move with him to Germany to live permanently. He even traveled to Germany, applied for my immigration, and prepared the paperwork for me to be admitted into Germany as a citizen. During his stay in Germany, Dr. Oskar also contacted my third brother, named Frederick, who lived in France.

When Frederick heard from Dr. Oskar, he wrote to me, so excited by the prospect of seeing me and Dr. Oskar in Europe. My former fiancé—from my arranged engagement when I was a teenager—also wrote to me. He had been sent to France to finish his doctoral studies and now lived there. Other relatives wrote and encouraged me to join them in Europe. Dr. Oskar insisted we bring Alex to Germany so the three of us could live together as a family.

One morning while I was at work, a young boy rushed up to me and told me that Soul had tried to kill himself.

By the time I got to Soul, several emergency rescue personnel were there with him. Soul lay on the ground, pale. His eyes were closed and his mouth was filled with water he drank while swallowing pills. His body seized.

Horrified, I saw a letter from Dr. Oskar nearby and knew what must have happened. Someone told me that they had seen Soul sitting alone and crying.

Emergency nurses and many others from the camp came to see what the commotion was about. Nurses started IV fluids to help him stabilize, but for several hours his body violently fought against medication.

The rumors spread throughout the whole camp about me, Soul, and Dr. Oskar. People spoke loudly enough that I could hear their comments about me being a scandalous woman. I considered myself a widow rejected by Soul's family, who would also make my son's life miserable. I loved Dr. Oskar, but it shattered me to see Soul like that.

Dr. Oskar had already left the camp for Germany to prepare documentation to take me with him. I didn't want to leave Soul like this, after all he had done for me. I didn't want to be the cause of this much pain for Soul. On the other hand, I loved Dr. Oskar. But I couldn't be with Dr. Oskar without hurting Soul. I was torn between the two.

When Soul woke, he told me how strong his feelings were for me and how afraid he was of losing me.

I had given up on someone who loved me so much. His attempted suicide changed my mind and I decided to stay with him instead of going to Germany with Dr. Oskar.

Soul, once again, had won my heart, and I made up my mind to stay with him. I couldn't bear to watch him die.

We still had occasional bombings nearby, with Khmer Rouge trying to challenge the People's Republic of Kampuchea military. Before he had left for Germany, Dr. Oskar had told me to go to another camp and wait for him if it became dangerous there.

When several bombs exploded close to where we were, Soul and I decided to move together to a different camp. Soon afterward, I became pregnant with Soul's child. During that time, I left my job in the German hospital ward and started a new job with UNICEF.

With a new dedication to Soul and our lives together, and knowing I would have another child, I decided to use the money I had saved to send for Alex. He had already lost his father; I wanted to reunite with him so we could resume our lives together. I had saved enough to bring him and my brothers and sisters so that we could all stay with each other at the camp.

The day they all arrived was the greatest time of my life. To have Soul, my son, and my siblings together again made my heart rejoice beyond anything I can describe with words.

About six or seven months later, Dr. Oskar hired a Khmer Red Cross worker to locate us. He found me when I was five months pregnant with Soul's child.

Dr. Oskar responded that he was willing to accept me. "I'll adopt your baby and take you all with me."

I told him of my commitment to Soul and my unborn child and declined his proposal.

Alex had already had to live without his dad, and I did not want to be the cause of another child not growing up with their biological dad.

I gave birth to a healthy baby girl. A coworker at UNICEF named her Mony. I had such a special bond with my father, that I vowed again to never separate Mony from her father.

It was clear to everyone that Soul and I had an amazing relationship. He loved us so much and was always by my side with his arm around me. I never had contact with Dr. Oskar again.

But, I had no idea what Soul had been hiding.

Chapter 18

BROKEN FAMILY, DESTINATION UNITED STATES

After losing so many family members, I cherished every moment with Alex and Mony. When it was time for me to go back to work at UNICEF, Soul took care of everything at home and I worked seven days a week from nine in the morning to five in the evening.

He was so attentive. After putting our baby to bed, Soul boiled water for me to take a warm bath, and then he gently dried me off.

One morning when I woke, I saw Soul in the shack a few feet away from ours. He was asleep and a Khmer woman lay next to him.

This had to be a dream.

I sat up. This was real. Soul and another woman were lying next to each other. The man who had warmed the water for my bath last night was in bed with another woman. We had fed our baby together before we put her to bed a few hours ago. How could he now suddenly start sleeping around?

My heart raced and my face heated. He had never hurt me. He had always held my hand and gone with me to places and had taken good care of me and my children. I had always trusted him. His love for me had always been my safe place.

How could I not know? I didn't suspect anything because he was home when I came home every evening. But, I realized I had no idea what he did while I was away at work. I had always trusted him.

In the following weeks, I learned Soul had started womanizing soon after I gave birth to our daughter.

Pangs of guilt entered my mind. Could he have done this to pay me back for the situation with Dr. Oskar? I had thought all that was behind us.

Or maybe he had started this after I decided to leave Dr. Oskar, thinking he no longer needed to prove his love to me.

The more I learned, I realized that ever since Mony came into our lives, instead of our relationship getting stronger, Soul had been growing away from me. He had made a lot of female friends and slept with several different women. Many told me that he cheated on me, and I should have left him. They said, "Once a cheater, always a cheater." But because he was always with me and my children every time I was home, I thought there was nothing to worry about.

I felt humiliated and abandoned. The tension caused my neck injury to flare up and my breast milk to diminish. Thankfully, I was able to get powdered milk from UNICEF.

1980

With skirmishes and unrest ongoing in Cambodia/Democratic Kampuchea, I remained under refugee status in the refugee camp. Because of my work with the Red Cross and UNICEF, the agencies allowed me to relocate to any country I chose when sponsors became available. I immediately chose Germany, the United States of America, or France.

When I considered choosing between those options I looked at any connection to communism. I saw what happened under communist rule in my country. I also remembered what I studied in college about Word War II, Hitler, and the communist movement there. They had suffered a holocaust and I had lived through my own. I remember hearing about the Berlin wall and the frightening history surrounding that.

With that information plus my firsthand knowledge of life under communism, I eliminated any European country with a connection to communism from my desired relocation list.

Even though I had no friends or family in the US, I decided to move there, for safety and freedom. Regrettably, I didn't think of Dr. Oskar in Germany or my brother Frederick in France, both of whom loved me and wanted me to relocate near them. I also had several good friends from school who now lived in France and wanted me to reunite with them. But, I had such painful memories of communism that nothing in Europe attracted me, especially Germany with its history of Nazism. All I could think of was getting my children to a safe place.

My sisters' minds were still polluted with anger toward me, so I didn't try to convince them to come with us. I asked my three brothers—Rick, Notch, and David—to come to the US with us.

I thought as long as Soul, Alex, Mony, and my brothers were with me, we should move to the US together. There, we would be safe from any communist regime, and my daughter would grow up having her biological father around.

How long could we live in a refugee camp waiting for a real job? We needed a fresh start to build a real life. We had always heard of the US as the land of opportunity. I filled out the paperwork and waited for sponsorship and our turn to be relocated.

I wished our family could have stayed together, but if I learned anything over the last few years, I knew some things were out of my control.

When they notified us we had a sponsor and were next to leave the refugee camp, my two younger brothers, Rick and Notch, decided to stay so they could be close to our sisters and their friends. I understood. They felt like they could protect them, and they had also established relationships there that would have been hard to break. I gave Rick and Notch some of my jewelry to sell if they needed to. David agreed to join us. He had lived with my husband and me when I first married. We had always been close.

Because Rick and Notch backed out of going, we had room for two more. Rick arranged for two of his friends to take his and Notch's place in the relocation. So, those two came with Soul, Alex, Mony, David, and me to live in the US, all hopeful for a life of peace and freedom.

As the plane took flight, I looked out a window. I already felt so far away from my younger siblings and wondered how they would manage the unfinished job regarding our parents' properties. I wished I had done more to take care of everything and to bring them to the US, especially Rick.

During the flight, I couldn't help but grieve over what we were leaving behind. My siblings were down there somewhere. My family. When would I be able to see them again?

If the king were still in power, and the war had not happened, our parents would have been so happy watching their children and grandchildren go into the businesses they had started. Our family would still be intact. These divisions would never have taken place. We would all be nearby one another and my parents would have lavished us with every privilege they could.

They had given us much more. Their blood still flowed through our veins and gave us strength and courage. I was left sobbing, with my heart torn to pieces. Though I left part of my family behind, their examples and their DNA still made me who I was. It was within me and within my siblings. We would always be family.

Chapter 19

STARTING OVER IN MASSACHUSETTS

During the first several months in the US, we lived in the very small town of North Easton in Massachusetts. Instead of happiness in a new, desirable, safe country, I felt a dark hole inside of me, insecure and sad. I started to miss my siblings, home, and family in Europe who loved and wanted me there. My heart went out to my children. Soul was no longer the same.

My emptiness repulsed me to the point that I lost the ability to think clearly. I ended up selling valuable jewelry left over from my mom and husband, especially my stunning diamond ring. It was mounted with 18-karat gold and nine big round pieces of select diamonds, which Mom, the gemstone expert, had selected. The marquis-shaped ring covered my whole index finger.

A Cambodian man caught me in a vulnerable, homesick moment and offered to pay only $500 for it. I knew that was far below market value, but being thousands of miles away from my siblings, it didn't seem to matter.

I had given some pieces to Rick and Notch before we left and had brought the rest with me, but now, in my heart, they represented the division in my family and I didn't want them around. I had a pair of diamond earrings with a big stone dropping down on both sides, shaped like an exclamation point. The four smaller stones on each bar led down to a larger stone that was close to half an inch wide. Both of those earrings were either lost or stolen.

After these were gone, I decided to put the rest of the jewelry in a safety deposit box at a bank in Brockton, Massachusetts, which I never remembered to bring with me. By the time I remembered, it was too late. What was left included several large and wide gold pieces, of which some were 24- and 18-karat gold bracelets and diamond necklaces my father had bought for me on a trip to Singapore. Other pieces were given to me at my wedding by my mother and my husband, Alex's father.

I wished I had given the remaining jewelry to Thyda. How did Thyda come to resent me so much? Was it all due to the propaganda we heard those years in the fields? Did it have something to do with the jewelry she returned to me when Mom died? Through all the events of the war, I had always expected our family to remain intact. If the jewelry caused her hatred toward me, I would gladly have given it to her.

* * *

Soul and I moved to Brockton. There we joined with a few fellow Khmer refugees including some we had known from the refugee camp. One woman invited Soul to her house.

Often.

When she talked to me, she reminded me of my closeness with Dr. Oskar at the Red Cross. She talked about how Soul tried to commit suicide because I had cheated on him. She chided me for wanting to be with a German doctor when Soul had been truly in love with me and she called me a scandalous woman.

Soul would always return to his daughter and me. I held on, thinking that at least Mony had a father.

He convinced me that he would stay with us rather than with his girlfriend. However, Soul had been traveling a lot. He met with several girlfriends.

I didn't understand. I was furious and hurt at the same time. I had trusted him and looked forward to living our lives together in the US. I had been warned about his cheating. Now, if I couldn't trust him, who could I trust? That undermined my ability to think rationally or function normally.

Almost two years later, Rick sent a letter asking to join us in the US. His new girlfriend, whom I hadn't met, had moved to the US. She called me and asked me to sponsor Rick. Hurt from the turmoil with Soul, and unsure of my future, I struggled to think of a way to help my brother on the other side of the planet.

Rick had given up his opportunity to come when I left. Now, I had no family or friends to rely on. The only people I knew to ask were my sponsors, but they didn't show any interest in helping me bring Rick to the US.

I agonized when he chose to stay and I had to leave him behind the first time. Now, I had no way to help him. My heart ached to help my younger brother, but I didn't know how. I felt so deeply sorry for not encouraging him more while we were together and for not being able to assist him now. I should have given him more big-sister direction while I was there with him.

After surviving so much in Cambodia, I thought life in the US would be wonderful. I had lived in fear of the Khmer Rouge. Now I lived in a foreign country and still didn't know whom to trust. I had two young children but had always had my extended family. Now, they were all so far away. Powerless to reunite us, a sense of failure sat heavily on my shoulders.

What did I do wrong?

I tried to keep our home going while Soul traveled. I took care of the children and tried to manage my fears of him rejecting me.

When Mony was about two years old, Soul didn't come home from his traveling. We waited and worried. She cried for her father and sat at the front door stairway to wait for him. My heart sank wondering if he would return to us.

I found out that he had a long-term Khmer girlfriend who was pregnant with his baby. Soon I found out that he had become a father to a girl with a woman who already had several children from her previous man.

He didn't return to us.

At that point, I felt he had made his life choice and I didn't want him back.

For a few years after Soul had left, I was so busy working and taking care of my children, I didn't notice David's eye. He had been injured during the war when he was on a work assignment for the Khmer Rouge one night and a thorn slapped him in the eye. It never healed and continued to bother him. I urged him to see a doctor about it.

The eye infection had become so gruesome that his eye had to be removed so the infection wouldn't affect his health. The eye surgery was hard on him. Even with the infection gone, he wasn't the same.

He moved closer to the Khmer community in Lowell, Massachusetts. I had no one to help me and my two children move, so he moved there by himself, leaving us alone.

* * *

One morning when I drove Mony to preschool, a car ran a red light and hit mine head-on. My head went through the windshield, and Mony flew from the backseat to the front. If she had been in the front seat, she would have surely died that day. The car was totaled.

Thankfully, Mony only suffered minor injuries. My neck and shoulders took the brunt of the impact, leaving me with ongoing bleeding down the back of my throat. At the time, I didn't know how to file insurance, so sadly I suffered from it all by myself.

A few years later, I headed to work at St. Elizabeth Hospital and became stuck in heavy traffic down the hill of Chelsea Bridge. Someone behind me rolled their vehicle and hit me from behind, denting the trunk lid and forcing my head against the windshield.

After a time of initial recovery, my neck refused to heal. Every time I turned my head, the pain took my breath. With this additional injury, my neck no longer had the strength to support the weight of my head. The searing pain only relaxed a little when I sat in a chair that supported my neck and head.

The cold winters in Massachusetts didn't help and clenched my neck. The stiffness magnified and the pain settled deeper in my bones and down into my shoulder blade.

Sleep evaded me. I struggled to find a position that eliminated enough pain to allow me to relax. Nights became a dreaded time of searching for rest but finding very little.

The darkness of night also found its way into my thoughts. The memories of such good times with my parents and siblings were harder to reach. I had been part of a vibrant family filled with love for one another. We worked together and gathered often.

During the war, we suffered together. Now, I suffered on the other side of the world, so far away from people who spoke my language and understood what I had been through. So far from my siblings and the beautiful country I had loved. Our home . . . the plantation . . . I understood why David had moved to the Khmer community, but I needed to keep my job to support my children.

Memories of the jungle, soldiers, and gunfire overshadowed the sweet memories and drew me into another spasm. The heartache of losing Pa, Mom, my husband, my siblings, and Soul drummed up tears that never ran dry. The physical pain and mental anguish created a nightly storm that denied me rest.

As restless hours passed, I became so afraid I would miss Alex's school bus, I didn't allow myself to sleep. I also knew I had to drive my daughter to her preschool. I had to take care of everyone. There was no one else to help me. The weight of the past while trying to establish a future fell heavily on my weary shoulders but my children gave me so much joy. We loved each other so much. Rick had always been there to help me, but now I lived on the other side of the world from him. I needed help but had no one.

I remembered walking with Mom away from our camp. She struggled but kept going even when she didn't think she could make it. She did all she could to keep us alive even when her body failed her.

Her same blood pulsed through my veins.

When sunlight crept through the windows, I managed to go through the motions of living. I told myself I would take care of my children as Mom did. The pain in my bones and in my heart wouldn't keep me from that.

A wake-up hug from Mony and a sweet smile from Alex gave me more strength than they realized. Thank You, Lord, for these children and wonderful companions. With You and them, I will press on.

1982

Life wasn't great; it wasn't even good, but I had to find a way to get past the feeling of being a lost sheep. I had to provide for my little family and make my way in this new place. With that lingering emptiness, I decided to go back to school. I attended Massasoit Community College where I made the dean's list. After that, I transferred to Northeastern University. When Alex was about six and Mony was one or two, I decided to transfer to Boston University, closer to my job at the hospital.

I learned of some well-paying federal jobs for bilingual workers and accepted a full-time position with St. Elizabeth Hospital in Allston/Brighton, Massachusetts. I worked with the WIC program as a nutrition counseling assistant, providing prenatal and toddler nutrition information. I had grown up with plenty of food and survived starvation, so it breathed life into my soul to be able to help someone. After living in the jungle scavenging for food to feed my family, I understood the desperation of these anxious mothers much more than they realized. My heart eased when I saw the relief come over their faces, knowing their children would have food.

I was so thankful to have a great, high-paying job. The hours were flexible and our secretary scheduled my client meetings around the time I needed to be with my children. A few years later, I was lucky enough to be able to accept another part-time job at the Lynn Courthouse as a victim witness assistant two days per week with almost the same salary as my full-time job at the hospital and getting off work at the same time as my children got out of school. I also worked as a substitute teacher occasionally. With a few jobs providing a good salary and flexible hours, I juggled university classes two evenings per week and still had quality time with Alex and Mony. It was physically hectic, but my children gave me so much strength and vitality to keep going.

For the first time in a long time, I felt the burden lifting and happiness emerging. My neck usually settled enough for me to get two or three hours of sleep at night in the long, cold Massachusetts winter. That wasn't enough sleep for a full rest, but it was better than complete exhaustion. It was the best time in our lives.

Chapter 20

I BECAME A CHRISTIAN AND MET PHILIP

Because of my long commute from Stoughton to Boston for work, a friend from church suggested I move to Boston. She babysat Alex and Mony and realized how much time my commute took from our day. She told me her daughter, Tanya, had a room for rent in that area. Alex, Mony, and I rented that room and moved in with her. She worked as a nurse on the night shift and babysat my children during the day until I got home from work and school.

Tanya expected me to cook for everyone and pay for food and rent long before the due date. I felt uneasy in the rough neighborhood with drug addicts on every street. I kept a close eye on Alex and Mony while I was with them but learned that some children hit Alex and Mony and they had been with people while they snorted cocaine.

For the sake of my children, I decided to move out of the neighborhood and that household. We stayed at a women's shelter for a couple of weeks, until I found an apartment to rent in Chelsey, Massachusetts.

Lesson learned.

I vowed to never take help from anyone or get another roommate.

We settled into our new apartment and our routine with school and work. I picked them up from school and took them home where a neighborhood high school kid that I'd hired would stop by each evening to babysit them, then I returned to work. We had one another. We had food and shelter. Life was good again.

Though I often drove home to check on the children, we finally felt somewhat safe. From time to time, I picked up my daughter from school and brought her back to work with me. We enjoyed spending time together. After work, we shopped for groceries. Both of my children did well in school and went into the gifted programs there.

I had a stable income, but those frigid winters took a heavy toll on me each year. My neck and shoulder pain escalated along with homework from my college classes and refused to let me sleep. Alex and Mony adapted to the cold with ease, usually with just one layer of clothing or blankets to keep them warm. I did not yet know how to layer my clothing to stay warm enough, so I barely managed the bitter cold, pain, and sleep deprivation.

At night, I waited in the cold for the train from Boston University. The chill penetrated my bones. My Cambodian blood couldn't adapt to the bitter Boston freeze and I ached from it.

I was aware that God had saved me from the killing fields, and I made a point of attending church to learn more about

Him and have a chance to meet more people. I had made a fresh start in the US but realized I needed to make a fresh start with my heart and soul. The more I learned about Jesus, the more I knew I needed His salvation. I prayed, accepted Him as my Savior, and was baptized in water. I had known of God, but now I fully believed that God was in my heart. I wanted to do all I could to follow His law.

Like many people, I had a lot to learn about living for Christ. My past trauma, my sins, and my selfish fears all distracted me. I met several young professionals who became Christian friends. They helped me and my children grow and learn.

As my fears diminished, friendships developed. I wasn't looking for a long-term relationship but dated a little. I dated a surgeon I met at St. Elizabeth Hospital. I also dated a coworker, an attorney I had met at Lynn Courthouse. He came to visit me and my children at our apartment. I remember giving him an inside plant with leaves that looked like marijuana. Everyone at work made jokes about it when he put it on his desk.

These Christian friends included me and my children in their families and leisure time. We often spent time studying the Bible together. We might not have been blood family, but we were very close.

Occasionally, my coworkers would get together for picnics and for holiday dinners. Among them was my friend Philip. He told me he had a job offer in Florida.

Florida. Warm, tropical weather. The thought of sunny winters made my heart flutter.

He invited me to join him.

We didn't know each other that well, but I listened. I believed some people from my hometown lived there. The thought of living in a warm climate enticed me. With my education and experience, I thought I could find a good-paying job, no matter where I moved. My children would have someone besides me. We would be safe and happy together and away from the bitter cold.

I thanked God for blessing me with good-paying jobs, a beautiful apartment, and precious Christian and professional friends. However, the neck and shoulder pain, along with insomnia, blinded me to making an impulsive decision before I asked for God's guidance. When Philip proposed, I accepted.

Alex urged me to stay in Massachusetts so he could finish his school there and follow his dream to attend MIT. Desperate to get us to a warm place where I could live without so much pain, I tried to assure him that he could pursue his dreams from anywhere.

I was so excited to escape the icy temperatures that I forgot to give notice at my three jobs or to say goodbye to my coworkers. I didn't even say goodbye to my friends or my landlord or notify my school.

Within a month, Philip and I were married at our friend Justin's house. The next day, Philip rented a U-Haul moving truck. Less than a week later, I got in the moving truck with my children and my cat by my side. We headed to Florida on what seemed like a great family adventure.

I should have seen the warning signs.

At the time, my brain was in a deep fog from chronic pain and my heart longed for sunshine, happiness, and a family.

I held on to those hopes so tightly that I didn't leave room to consider the uncertainty that loomed over us. It didn't occur to me that I would be dragging my children into something far different from the fantasy I envisioned.

Alex was not happy about leaving. Philip was a sport about it all and tried to calm Alex. The cat made a huge fuss about the ordeal, matching the grumpiness of my son. But we headed south and arrived in the Sunshine State in one piece and full of hope.

Philip worked at the Greyhound bus office in Orlando. Then they transferred him to Jacksonville, where we lived for a year. Those first two years of life with Philip were good. This man who rescued me from the brutal northern winters loved me, and I loved him. He was great with the children and accepted them as his own.

He ended up losing the position in Jacksonville, so we lived off my bank account. I knew that wouldn't be sustainable and that I needed to find work.

I decided to finish my degree in computer technology. Some classes transferred from Boston. But to get a job sooner, I changed to a shorter, faster technical skill program. No credits transferred for that program. I had to take the entire course. Soon after I graduated from the electronic technology program, we had to move again, this time to Columbia, South Carolina. Philip had been accepted into the PhD program at USC.

After our third move in two years, I began to realize that this was not the dream I had in mind. God had saved me from the Khmer Rouge and car accidents. He had provided me means to earn a good living, Christian friends, and the blessing of children, but now, in another new place without a job or friends, grief settled around me and in me. I began to question myself. How could I have been so selfish to be drawn to Florida when my family had so much before? How could I have made such a serious mistake? Why didn't I ask God or listen to my son and talk with my Christian friends before I made that drastic decision? It all happened so quickly. Because of the moves and our current situation, I was not able to fulfill my son's wish to attend MIT.

I agonized that I made a selfish decision without God. I determined to spend more time reading my Bible and in prayer. God assured me that He would never leave me or forsake me.

Chapter 21

STARTING OVER IN SOUTH CAROLINA

1988
South Carolina

Philip wanted to live in the dorm at USC, so I decided to buy a house in West Columbia, to be in a better situation for the children. Without Philip at home with us, I had to care for their needs alone. I found a job.

Philip was about a year into grad school when he told me he had to travel to prepare for his thesis to get his PhD. One cold December afternoon, I received a big envelope in my mailbox. I opened the bulky envelope and read through the stack of legal papers. Philip wanted a divorce.

I held on to the kitchen countertop to keep my balance. He had given me no clue—no discussions about us or even a phone call to explain his feelings to me. He wanted my signature to end our marriage.

When the shock lightened, I became so angry, not to mention disappointed. I learned he had moved to North Carolina and met a Korean woman there. He was in love with her.

Stunned and hurt, I had little choice but to sign the papers and to be strong for my children. As my parents had done for me, I would do all I could to protect and care for my children and move forward, no matter what happened.

Panic set in when I found out Philip had taken the remaining funds from my bank account. I owned a house but had little income. Alex and Mony depended solely on me, so I applied for government assistance. Unfortunately, owning a home disqualified us from the assistance programs.

I felt like Philip had dropped us off in the middle of the ocean with no paddle. I read the Bible passage in Isaiah 60 about being "forsaken and hated with no one passing through" (v. 15 NASB 1995). I thought, *That's me, God. That's exactly how I feel.*

Then I read the remaining portion of verse 15. "I will make you an everlasting pride, a joy from generation to generation." From the surrounding text, I understood the promise was for the Jewish people, but it gave me comfort, as one of God's people, to know He understood. God is the only one who rules the entire universe—"From one man he made all the nations, that they should inhabit the whole earth" (Acts 17:26)—and I could do this with Him. Alex and Mony were my next generation, and they depended on me.

I knew God would be with me to direct my path, and my children were my paddle to move forward. With a renewed determination, I scanned newspapers for job opportunities. In 1988, before computers, cell phones, and the internet were so widespread, it was a challenge to find career openings as well as prepare for the requirements that came with them. With no money, I was ready to take any work just so I could pay bills and buy food. We were broke.

I had my faith and my children but still struggled. The climate wasn't as warm as the one we had in Florida, but at least it wasn't the bitter cold of Massachusetts. Then again, I had good jobs and good friends there. We had Asian markets in the north, but it was frustrating for me to shop in most grocery stores in Columbia. I didn't know how to cook American cuisine, and they didn't stock what I needed for my Asian meals. I felt like the only Asian in the area. I met some Filipinos but no one who spoke Khmer. The feeling of isolation drained my strength. I missed my jobs and my friends from Massachusetts.

I didn't have time for self-pity but instead focused on our basic needs. I let Alex and Mony ride the bus to school so I could work. When helplessness tried to overwhelm me, God reminded me, "These things I have spoken to you, so that in Me you may have peace. In the world you have tribulation, but take courage; I have overcome the world" (John 16:33 NASB 1995).

The peace He gave me during those days gave me the strength to look for the sunrise the next day and go on. I felt an assurance that as He had been with me years ago, He would be with me for all my tomorrows.

I watched as Alex and Mony settled into the neighborhood and rode their bicycles after school. I remember the joy of seeing them play and make friends with the children in the neighborhood.

Both children did extremely well in school and the teachers raved about their progress. I knew they were both talented and smart. It was nice that the school system recognized it too.

Mony told her teacher that I was her best friend. That was the ultimate compliment for me. God truly blessed me with these smart and precious children. I was incredibly grateful.

I remember at my parents' house being so spoiled. I never learned how to cook because they hired cooks. When they rang the bell, I came to the dining room to eat. We sat around the table as a loving family, enjoying delicious meals.

I had tried to learn how to cook and improvise with ingredients I found in American stores. It was nothing like my childhood food with fresh fish, fruits, and vegetables, but I improvised and managed. My children ate whatever I made for them.

My parents had given us so much then and prepared us for our futures. I had to do the same for my children. We struggled more than most families, but we took time to celebrate little moments of joy. It hurt my soul to know they would never sit with my parents and siblings at that table, but I tried to give them as much love as I could.

While thankful for my job, I still needed more income. Working all day and taking care of the children at night left me little opportunity to search for more work. Most jobs required physical labor. My multiple neck injuries made that work almost as bad as the rice fields. Shocked and surviving in emergency mode, my brain didn't think to look for a job with my degree. We urgently needed a paycheck.

I took a job as a waitress. Customers graciously left me tips, but the stress from the job mounted. Sleep evaded me. Aching from the work, my mind refused to settle down. I relived the Khmer Rouge soldier beating me. I cried again for Pa and Mom. I thought about my prince, my husband, and the years in the rice fields. Bags formed under my eyes and weariness clung to me like an anchor.

When I came home after midnight, my children were asleep. I sat by their beds and cried over them in silence. I kissed my fingertips and lightly placed them on their heads. I wouldn't wake them or let them see me cry. At least they could rest.

I found ways to shop frugally and bought only bargains. If I learned anything from the Khmer Rouge, it was that I could push my body to work harder than I thought I could. But those years left scars and injuries that hindered my best efforts to push myself. Yet, in those restless nights, I determined to gather enough strength to overcome absolutely anything. God was with me. He had been for a long time.

Alex and Mony never complained that I wasn't there to help with their homework or buy them gifts. They understood money was tight. They even helped me by doing their laundry and cleaning. My parents had maids and cooks and showered us with protection, love, and luxury. I couldn't give my children luxury, but we were together and I loved them with every cell of my being. We were a team that could take on anything, whether it was big or small. We never stopped moving forward.

1990

Many things had gone wrong since leaving Massachusetts. We had moved three times in two years, finally settling in Columbia, South Carolina. Because I was never able to use my skills from electronic technology or from my previous job, I decided to return to the medical field. I applied to and was accepted in the surgical technology program at the local community technical college.

After two years of instruction and one year of clinical work, my classmates and I went to our graduation and celebrated our success together. A few days later, I opened my graduation folder and found it empty. I called my clinical instructor. She informed me that my education was "incomplete" and invited me back to repeat my year of clinical work.

I didn't understand what was happening, but I accepted her offer, hoping to get hired by the hospital. All of my classmates had already accepted jobs and moved to other hospitals. I didn't want to be left behind.

Soon after classes ended, my original classroom instructor retired and moved out of town. He did not attend our graduation. A few months later, my clinical instructor passed away and all of my classmates were gone, so no one was aware of what had happened to me. I ended up working full-time in clinical operations without an instructor around to guide me. Nevertheless, I did well and got along with the full-time hospital employees, even without the clinical instructor there to see how well I did.

I often worked during semester breaks, which was very unusual for students, and volunteered to substitute without pay for vacationing employees. But, repeating that year of clinical work did me no good. I really didn't understand what was happening. I was a good student, continually scoring *A*s and *B*s, and yet I was given no explanation for not graduating with my classmates. It was an absolute nightmare because of the amount of stress I was under in school and out. During my school tenure, I had married a man named Ted and was facing a toxic in-law who constantly berated me. I simply couldn't do it anymore.

I had been so excited at the graduation ceremony with all of my classmates. In the end, however, it turned out this was not to be the career for me. God had chosen a different road for me to travel. I just didn't know what it was yet.

* * *

God had been with us every step of the way and sent people to help us. Our neighbor Ted was one of those people.

Ted was twenty-eight and single. Before Alex went to university, he, Mony, Ted, and I attended church together. He enjoyed spending time with my children when I was at work. I trusted him because they enjoyed their time with him and got along so well. Ted helped me fix things around our house. It was good to have such a kind young man I could count on. We gradually became good friends.

When my divorce from Philip was finalized, Ted and I decided to go out together. I enjoyed seeing Alex and Mony get along with him so well. Alex encouraged us and supported the relationship.

Since they were so comfortable together, I let Ted watch my children more often. I almost felt like they loved Ted more than me. No matter what happened, they truly loved Ted. For a few years after my divorce from Philip, Ted helped support us. Having a house next to him was the best thing I could think of about moving to South Carolina.

Five years of friendship turned into a wedding proposal. I never knew I would marry my best friend, but I did.

Unlike my impulsive marriage to Philip, Ted and I discussed everything before we married. I was in school full time in the surgical technology program. We discussed our finances. He had a lot of credit card bills to pay, and I needed to finish school to get a good job. We decided I would sell my house and we would move in with him. We would use the money from the sale of the house to pay off his credit card bills. After graduation I would find a job, and we would start financially together from scratch.

In 1993, about a year before I completed my surgical technology program, Ted and I married. Everyone who attended our wedding at our church thought that I was lucky, marrying a man who had never married before and had no children of his own.

Alex finished his last year of high school and earned a scholarship to an Ivy League school. He left to attend the University of Pennsylvania. Mony, who was five years younger than Alex, and I stayed home with Ted.

1995

Just after our second wedding anniversary, in 1995, Ted, Mony, and I took a trip to France to visit Charnay, my youngest sister, and two of my brothers, Frederick and Notch. I was hoping this trip to see my family would rejuvenate my strength as I was having a terrible time dealing with stresses at home. Instead, it just added to them.

When we arrived, my younger sister, who stayed close to Thyda in the camp during the Khmer Rouge, was in France. Unfortunately, instead of being happy to see me, she still expected me to be the giver, like a mother, and provide for her needs. It was a good thing my brother Frederick, who had been living in Europe long before the war, understood the turmoil I was going through. However, my younger sister did not. Yes, of course I wanted to be a big sister and be able to provide for everyone's needs, both emotionally and financially; however, I couldn't take care of them by myself. In fact, they were doing much better than my children or me. I was glad to see everyone doing well, but I was hurt that some of them still hated and blamed me.

The trip did not have the rejuvenating effect I had hoped.

Chapter 22

TRIALS WITH BERTHA

For they cannot rest until they do evil;
they are robbed of sleep till they make someone stumble.

—Proverbs 4:16

Ted grew up in a dysfunctional family. I didn't learn the full story until many years later, but during our first year of marriage, he warned me about his mother.

On a trip to his parents' house when it was just the two of us, he said, "Dad moved into a trailer to get away from Mom several years ago. He has cancer now and has moved back in with her, but I really don't understand why."

Ted repeated himself in a soft tone of voice that he just didn't understand why his dad had moved back in with his mom.

I said, "Maybe he is too sick to take care of himself now. Maybe that's why."

Ted said, "It's just hard for me to be around her, knowing she'll be critical of everything."

I asked why he would say such a thing.

"You have to understand, Vera." He then explained that she favored her younger son and his family. For instance, she never sat down to eat without them. On the other hand, she never waited for Ted to arrive before eating. If he came late, the grandchildren had already made a mess of the food. He also said that he got so nervous around the children that he felt he would have a heart attack.

"Wow. I'm sorry."

It was hard for me to imagine that scenario after having such love and respect in my home. At the time, my children and I desperately wanted to have an extended family, and Alex and Mony were excited to have someone to call grandma, so I chalked his ramblings up to exaggeration. I didn't pay much attention to his warning. As it turns out, Ted was afraid to tell me and my children the truth about how his mother treated him. (It would take several more years for him to do so.) Ted's laid-back, soft-spoken personality can be frustrating. His anxiety and nervousness prevented him from standing up for me and my children. Maybe that added to the pressure I was under. I felt I had no one to fight for us.

I wish I had known then what I know now. Maybe I could have been better prepared to stay away from her, to protect my children, to tell my children the truth. I was blinded by my own mistake and found it hard to believe that she could act in the way Ted was describing. But with Ted's father's illness, her grandchildren loving to play with me and following me everywhere I went, and my previous mistake of not listening to my son when he warned me against moving (and subsequently missing out on attending MIT), I was so afraid to say anything to anyone and didn't want to disappoint my Alex and Mony because both of them loved Ted and his family. I didn't want my children to get worried and possibly do poorly in school. I did not want to rock the boat, so I swallowed my pride too long until everything had gotten out of control.

During the first five years of our marriage, Alex and Mony would join Ted's family only during the holidays. That was the only time my children would see Bertha, and everyone had a great time. So very few people were aware of how bad she treated me. My children knew nothing of her abuse.

Ted's parents lived a little over an hour's drive away from us. During our weekend visits with his parents, Ted stayed busy teaching his dad about their new home computer. This was the mid '90s, and home computers were still new and exciting. Besides, they couldn't do much in the way of physical activity since the cancer had progressed to the point he was in a wheelchair and on oxygen.

While Ted occupied himself with his dad, I stayed with his mom and her younger son's children, whom, it seemed, she couldn't live without. They seemed to be her first priority before anyone else, including her ailing husband. I helped Bertha with cooking, cleaning, and taking care of the grandchildren. They were small and I enjoyed spending time with them.

It didn't take long for Bertha's attitude toward me to change. Nothing I did seemed to please her. No matter what I did, she shot stinging critical remarks toward me. I was in school finishing my degree, but she criticized me for that, saying I should be working instead.

Ted doesn't talk much and didn't tell her I was taking classes to get a good job and had sold my house, paying off his debts. He told me, "I can't change my mom."

We continued our weekly visits, but it was misery. I tried to please her, but she made a point of seating me in the kitchen with the grandchildren, away from the adults in the dining room. She didn't even include me in family pictures.

Her life revolved around her favorite son, his wife, and their children, and she made a point of telling everyone about him. People who attended church with Bertha told us that they never heard anything from her about Ted. Even when it was just us, her first comments to us were always about how wonderful and important her younger son and his children were to her. I heard it so much that when I went to bed at night, I could still hear her voice talking about her grandchildren in my head. It was extremely uncomfortable to be around her, to hear her bragging so much about her younger son right in front of Ted.

She had hounded Ted to remain single so he could care for his parents and younger brother and his family. Now he had married me, but she seemed to expect Ted to give her money instead of spending it on us. She even wanted us to make our wills with her as the beneficiary. At the time, we had no assets except Ted's small house. I never intended to take advantage of Ted, but his mother thought otherwise.

She accused me of taking everything Ted had away from her and her grandchildren—"Without you, he would stay single." She added that if he had stayed single, he could have passed everything down to her younger son instead of us.

> Hear my cry for help,
> my King and my God,
> for to you I pray.
> In the morning, LORD, you hear my voice;
> in the morning I lay my requests before you
> and wait expectantly.
>
> —Psalm 5:2–3

For about five years while his dad was so sick, we were at their home nearly every weekend. I did everything I could think of to honor Bertha, hoping that she would accept my children as her own. I didn't care how bad she treated me as long as she would accept them as her own grandchildren. I was willing to sacrifice everything I had for that to happen. But, the harder I tried the more she pushed us away. I cooked and cleaned. Whatever needed to be done, I jumped in and helped, hoping it would bring about a change of heart from her. When it became hard to remain civil toward her, God reminded me, "Love your enemies, do good to those who hate you" (Luke 6:27 NASB 1995). I also prayed Psalm 4:1:

> Answer me when I call to you,
> my righteous God.
> Give me relief from my distress;
> have mercy on me and hear my prayer.

When Ted's father was hospitalized and it was clear that he was nearing the end of his life, Bertha asked Ted to stay with his dad at the hospital and she asked me to come with her to buy clothes for his dad's burial. Instead of shopping, though, she took me to clean her younger son's house. After cleaning, she snatched things from my hand and expressed how unhappy she was with me and my innocent Mony. She made it so clear that she would never accept us. It was an ongoing thread of rejection, enough to fry my brain. I doubted my ability to think, and it pulled me into an unending pit of sorrow. She was extremely depressing to be around.

A while after Ted's father died, Bertha told me how much she had hated her husband. "He kept us poor working at that glass factory. We had no washer or dryer. We didn't have modern appliances."

She never ran out of ways to try to split our family and specifically hurt me. She even reintroduced Ted to his old girlfriend—at his uncle's funeral. The old girlfriend introduced herself to me and we talked while Bertha sat staring daggers at us.

Bertha got a boyfriend not long after her husband died. She told me that she would not marry him until he kicked his children out of his own home. She told me that she had been in fights with them and would like to see them in jail. What she described was exactly how I felt she had treated me and my children.

Almost every morning after Ted left for work, Bertha called me, screaming in a hostile tone, "Put Mony to work. Get both your butts out there and get a job." She always hung up before I had a chance to say anything.

With good reason, Ted was reluctant to be around his mom. I thought maybe I was the problem and offered to stay home and let him go spend time with her if he thought that would be easier. He refused.

His coworkers told me to be gentle with Ted. He was a hard worker and always in his shell, but he always relied on his physical strength rather than mental strength. I looked at it as Ted trusting God to handle what he couldn't.

Like David wrote in Psalm 38:13–15:

> But I, like a deaf man, do not hear;
> And I am like a mute man who does not open his mouth.
> Yes, I am like a man who does not hear,
> And in whose mouth are no arguments.
> For I hope in You, O Lord;
> You will answer, O Lord my God. (NASB 1995)

Bertha's bitterness escalated after the death of Ted's father, and with every passing year, I understood more of why Ted had been so hesitant to spend time with her. I wanted to be a good daughter-in-law, but my irritation grew from her continual rejection of us and comparison of Ted to her younger son.

My children still referred to Bertha as "Grandma." It never occurred to them how badly she treated me behind everyone's back. Bertha seemed to have two personalities: she was cruel to me when no one was around, but her personality changed immediately when someone walked by.

Though I had a hard time understanding Bertha, God understood. The Bible speaks of people who seem to need to hurt people: "For they cannot rest until they do evil; they are robbed of sleep till they make someone stumble."

It infuriated Bertha to see that Ted loved me and my children and that he would not bow to her demands. So she used a different tactic. She accused me of using Ted for his money. She didn't know I had sold my home and we used that money to pay off his debts.

Her unfounded hatred reminded me of my time in the killing fields. I still tried to win her over in different ways. She told me she wanted a certain expensive diamond necklace, so I bought it for her. She never wore it but gave it to her grandchildren.

I thought she might warm up to me if I called her "Mom." But Ted's sister informed me that I "should not call her Mom. She's not your mom." At the same time, some of Bertha's other relatives told me how horribly she talked about me. They were not happy with the situation, but there was nothing they could do to stop her.

Bertha asked me to come with her to a quiet place and brought several envelopes filled with pictures of her favorite son's children and handed them to me. "Here. You need to put these in your house."

Dumbfounded, I took the envelopes. She had their pictures in every room of her house, but I didn't plan to. Hoping to pacify her, I smiled and took them. When she found out I didn't do what she asked, she became furious.

A few years after my children left and soon after Bertha's grandchild had a baby, she demanded that Ted and I adopt her great-grandchildren. She would say this even in front of other people. When other relatives would hear my refusal, they would clap their hands in front of her and say, "Enough is enough! Ha, Vera!"

Of course I would love to adopt any children who need help and need a place to live, but why would I adopt her grandchildren when she was making it impossible for me to parent my *own* children? Even though we told her we wouldn't, Bertha pressured us to adopt them every time we saw her

She was frustrating and exhausting to be around.

Ted and I got so numb that we no longer paid attention to her. We both wanted to live in peace and give respect to his mother. I suppose she felt that I hurt her by taking Ted away from her, so she wouldn't rest until she had driven a wedge between our family.

I often prayed the Psalms of David for solace and comfort. For example:

> Hear me when I call, O God of my righteousness!
> You have relieved me in my distress;
> Have mercy on me, and hear my prayer."
>
> —Psalm 4:1 NKJV

And, "You have removed lover and friend far from me; my acquaintances are in darkness" (Psalm 88:18 NASB 1995).

I wanted to obey God's command to forgive those who persecuted us. Bertha's hurtful words and manipulation came like bullets every day and became nightmares at bedtime as I lay awake worrying. Ted worked long hours and was hardly home enough to see what was going wrong.

Bombarded with continual mental abuse from Bertha, I tried again to please her. Although Mony was only thirteen, I sent her out after school to work as Bertha continued to demand.

One night, after her first babysitting job, Mony disappeared for several hours. I searched for her, desperate to find my daughter but with no way to reach her. I panicked, worrying something had happened to her. I don't know where she was during those hours, but I suspected that something bad had happened while she was gone. She returned that morning. While I drove her to school, I saw she had cut her wrist, trying to commit suicide.

She refused to tell me why.

My whole body trembled with indescribable disbelief. Instead of wrapping my arms around her and supporting her, I got so panicked and was unable to think. My broken spirit wept for my child's safety. To see my little Mony hurt shocked my heart and broke my hope of seeing my child do well in school. I couldn't cry in front of her; instead I became an enraged animal and hurled caustic remarks toward her. It must have been an emotional breakdown from the anger and frustration of the constant verbal abuse from Bertha. I was unable to stand up for my child or to protect her. Ted was always at work; we had just moved to the area so I had no one to share the pain of my situation with Bertha. All I had was my little Mony, who was the only person close to me. I honestly didn't mean to aim any anger and frustration at my poor innocent child, but my action irritated her. She didn't understand what was going on; my child misunderstood and it became an ongoing issue among us. Afterward, Mony was no longer the child I used to have. She left home a couple of times without telling me where she was staying. We filed missing persons reports with the police, and I asked Ted to place her picture everywhere in the neighborhood, but we still had no answer. Both Alex and Mony were exceptionally brilliant children, but due to anxiety and emotional challenges from me, Mony was unable to finish high school and, instead, later got a GED. My soul was so depleted; I had hurt my child, and it became a problem for the rest of our lives.

My behavior caused Mony to change too. She had been remarkably talented—brilliant. But her behavior at school completely changed. My heart broke thinking of how I had let her down. My stress and depression were so great that I could no longer hold a job. Bertha had also accused me of using Ted's income. Without my income and with all of the other stressors combined, I screamed at Alex when he came to me asking for help with his tuition. I spiraled into a deeper agonizing depression, which made my relationship with my children even worse. They didn't understand and no longer wanted to be near me.

The stress of dealing with Bertha's abuse, Mony dropping out of school, losing my job, hormonal imbalances, a miscarriage, and insomnia made me defensive and left me drained. Ted worked late all the time, which fueled my anger against him for not standing up for his wife and children. And Bertha continued spending a lot of time exploring ways to destroy us.

A few years later, when Mony was fifteen, she returned home. Almost every week Bertha called Ted to check up on us and learned that Mony had returned to us and learned how to drive. Bertha immediately called me and in a vicious tone of voice tried to convince me that if Mony got into a car accident, Ted might lose his house. She told us not to let her drive. Here again, she told me how Ted had worked so hard to take care of us.

I let it all build up inside of me from the first year I was married to Ted until the first time Mony ran away from home at age thirteen.

Neither Ted nor I had the willpower to stop this monster. Instead of taking steps to protect my children against Bertha, who was affecting our marriage and my emotional balance, we held back. I honestly couldn't count on Ted; he didn't want to get close to or face his mother and didn't share my sorrows. Ted had a lot of anxiety and nervousness and couldn't deal with obstacles like these.

Chapter 23

NOT HER BLOOD!

Not a word from their mouth can be trusted;
their heart is filled with malice.
Their throat is an open grave;
with their tongues they tell lies.

—Psalm 5:9

My daughter had run away more than once while Alex was away at school. Seven years later, after a stint in the Peace Corps, Alex returned home to advance his skill in accounting. At the same time, my daughter had come back and all three of us were together in my husband's house. I was incredibly happy to see both back home with me, together again. I felt that I was one of the luckiest people on earth. I had missed them very much. But my happiness would not last long.

The minute Bertha found out that my Alex and Mony were back home with me, she became enraged. Without letting us know, she drove sixty miles to our house and barged in the front door.

> *Among which I scatter you,*
> *I will not completely destroy you.*
> *I will discipline you but only in due measure;*
> *I will not let you go entirely unpunished.*
> . . . .
> *There is no one to plead your cause,*
> *no remedy for your sore,*
> *no healing for you.*
> *All your allies have forgotten you;*
> *they care nothing for you.*
>
> —Jeremiah 30:11, 13–14

After she saw all three of us together, she didn't say anything in front of my children; however, without letting my children hear, she asked me to take a ride with her in her car. I went. When it was just the two of us, with a very harsh and loud and angry tone of voice, she told me that my children were "not her blood." She spit at my face, yelling, "They are not my blood!" This time she had gone too far, she was determined that the children would be out of Ted's house. She pushed me to the edge; she knew my weaknesses. After I had put up with this for seven years, these words were as strong as a knife stabbing me. It was to the point that I was not able to maintain self-control. I was immediately blinded to the point that I exploded in front of my own innocent children. What a life-changing mistake! Without my children understanding the truth, my action backfired on me. I regretted not being able to tell them what was really going on. I was afraid that if I did tell them, they would be angry with me because they loved Ted and his family.

Suddenly some sort of dark energy completely blocked me and caused me to lose my true identity. It was not the real me. I was not sure who I was. I had misdirected my anger toward Bertha onto my own children instead.

As she had done many times before, she drove me away from my children and made sure no one was around as a witness. I allowed this to affect me to the point that it blinded me. I then manifested those pent-up feelings toward my children. That turned out to be the last day my innocent children and I were under the same roof.

Bertha had manipulated me for several years, and I had kept it all inside. After she injected her toxic words into my head on this day, she dropped me off without saying goodbye to my children or Ted. The words "not her blood" were as sharp as a knife and stabbed at my chest. Suddenly, seven years of pent-up fury, seven years of denial and antagonism, seven years of concealed abuse popped like a balloon in my children's faces. I screamed loudly, and an evil voice came from my gut in front of my poor teenagers. My burning flame was hysterical and burst onto my innocent children. Without knowing what was going on, both children thought that I was angry at them, and they started to scream back at me. We ended up fighting with one another while Ted stood there looking at us. He never said a word.

The next morning, the burning flame continued among us. Deep inside my heart I felt nothing but love for them, but they thought otherwise due to my long-term irrationality. My children no longer wanted to be with me; they said I was toxic to them. Unexpectedly, Alex packed to leave and told me he would not return. That same day, Mony ran away from home. It would be the last time I saw my children for many years. I ached to my very soul as my heart was shattered. God knows how bad I felt that day. I felt as though I were in an unending pit of sorrow to see my innocent children with no one to stand up for us. Unfortunately, Ted was too fragile to stand up to his mother.

It reminded me of when I was separated from my family during the Khmer Rouge. In both instances, we had been separated for so long but were finally back together. I was full of hope that we could make a fresh start, but forces converged to pull us apart again. For my mother, that force was death. For my children, it was me.

I once again felt intense grief in every pore of my body. I never thought I would feel a pain worse than losing my mother, but I was wrong. This was worse. I knew that my relationship with my children was over. I once again fell into a pit of sorrow, but this time, it was a pit of my own making.

Unlike my mother, who I knew had lived her final days in peace and freedom, my children were now alone—on the streets—and I lost the ability to help them. I was confused, and they hid from me, refusing to let me know where they were. They used to cling to me as their mother; now I was practically a stranger to them. I was no longer their best friend. I had no comfort when I thought about where they were. I got no relief from my thoughts and guilt. I had watched Alex weep over my mother's grave when we lost her. Did he weep for me now? I know I wept for both of them. I had driven my children away, and now they were out there, moving from place to place, scared to come back home.

They were alone in the world with all kinds of strangers. It was tragic that they both left me so soon and too young to take care of themselves, especially Mony. I don't know when my girl became a woman. I never had time to train her to become a housewife; life was so hectic that I never had a chance to teach her how to cook. Alex and Mony had no personal coaching as to how to live a normal life. My actions were the mistake of a lifetime. At their age they should have had their mother to comfort and guide them, but I had destroyed that.

After my children left, I was in a dangerous state of trauma. I wondered if I had the physical and mental stamina to carry on. I trembled not knowing where to find them; I sobbed through the darkness of the night so utterly empty. I awaited the dawn that would bring hope, but brokenness hung over me.

There was none to guide her.

—Isaiah 51:18

My defenses caused me to build high walls between Ted and me. I became like an animal backed into a corner. I felt like no one wanted to be my friend, and the few I had turned away from me. They made fun of me, telling me that they felt so bad for Ted for being married to a mentally disturbed lunatic. Combine these two sentences to read, "I suffered a miscarriage that, combined with hormonal changes and a thyroid issue, flung me into an even deeper pit of depression." My personality changed; I had premenopause and empty-nest syndrome. I had failed too often.

No matter what I was doing, my mind was always with them—every hour, every day. I prayed for healing and restoration. I would wake up with nightmares, wondering what happened to them. When I ate, I wished to have them sitting at the table eating with me. Without them by my side, life was utterly empty and without meaning. I so missed having them around and worried all the time. I couldn't even watch the news on TV. Every time I saw a report of a rape or a murder, I was afraid this bad thing had happened to them. I was full of regret and felt as though I was living in the darkness of hell.

Without my children, there was a dark hole inside my soul. I was in pain without them. All I could do now was pray that God would be with them always. I surrendered to and accepted that God was in charge.

Immediately I started to put my foot down against Bertha, but it was too late. My children were already gone. I started to hate Ted and his family. I blocked them out of my life, and I regretted selling my first home. But Bertha never gave up. All she cared about was having me take care of her younger son's family. No matter how many times I refused, she ignored me, and it became very clear that she expected me to acknowledge her and her grandchildren and to accept my defeat. Bertha was extremely selfish; her conquest became my tears and my ultimate loss.

* * *

God knows, I wish I was able to express what happened that day and why. Obviously, the years of manipulation and strong emotional pain had broken my spirit and my heart. I was choked with enormous hurt. I angered both my children, driving them away.

I never realized how much I needed my children, my family, and my relatives. I have many regrets and much remorse about how I responded to them. It was unacceptable. At that moment I was worse than an animal toward them, I was unable to rationalize right from wrong. Those words, *not her blood,* and those painful memories trouble my children and me to this day. From that point on, I felt like the walking dead, a zombie.

When my children left, I fell into a place of darkness, which lasted for more than twenty-five years. Without Mony and Alex, there was a big hole inside of my heart. No matter what happens to us, they are more precious than gold to me, and nothing can replace them. Nonetheless, both still had resentment toward me and thought that I wanted to kick them out of the house or didn't want them with us. Neither Alex nor Mony had a clear picture of how bad Bertha acted toward me. Without knowing the truth, my children held it against me. They thought that I was too toxic to be around, that I was a bad mother to them. They still thought nothing was wrong with Bertha.

These horrible memories shake me to the core and char my restless mind. Today and every day, I long for a full restoration in all of our lives, scattering and gathering. God rescues us during our trials and tribulations. In His providence, no matter where my children are, I earnestly pray for

God to be with them, to defend them, and to protect them from any harm and from any danger.

Sometimes, it seemed easier to have survived three years in the killing fields, where a million people died, than to see my innocent children in the street with no one to help them. When we needed help, I felt we were invisible to my mother-in-law. Ultimately, I forgave her, but there was too much bitterness and long-term destruction to me and my children. My marriage and my business were affected.

My emotional traumas were piling up, way beyond repair; therefore, I no longer wanted contact with Ted's family. At the same time, my children wanted no contact with me. Even though I tuned Ted's family out, I encouraged Ted to keep in touch with his family without me. He would always say "absolutely not" every time I asked.

When he saw me in a deep depression after my children left, he decided to write them a letter to explain how bad his mother had been toward us, but it was too little too late. On top of that, it took him many more years to finally tell me more about his childhood. He finally told me, "In our house, while I was growing up, they were constantly screaming at each other. It was first thing I heard when I woke up in the morning. I once saw my dad hit my mother on the back of her head with a shovel." I knew Ted genuinely cherished us, but the violent words and actions he saw when he was young affected him. He retreated from conflict, becoming nervous. He didn't talk about it, but those wounds lingered in him. Unfortunately, the whole thing changed Ted's personality for his entire life.

I felt that Ted had heard Bertha speak unkindly to me, but he didn't stand up for himself or protect us. I realized that while I'm shell-shocked from war, he's shell-shocked from his family. He's uncomfortable around strangers and hesitant to make new friends.

Even now, thirty years later, those wounds aren't healed. Deep in my heart I know that Ted loved us and trusted me to make all the decisions, so I was willing to do that. Many times over the thirty years, I have encouraged Ted to honor Bertha's wishes and to try to form a closer bond with his mother, but it never worked. I even was willing to permanently let him go, but he refused and asked me to stay away from his family completely. From the time that his dad died, Ted isolated himself from his family. Bertha is the only person who calls to check on him. If he finds out that I've called his aunt or cousin, he tells me to leave all of them alone and to contact no one in his family. Ted is a lonely man, but he took us in and stood by me, and our marriage has lasted this long because Ted is a very honest person. He's always been very quiet and laid back no matter how frustrated I got.

Bertha's toxic behavior caused too much damage to us. She lied, manipulated people, and was delusional, deceptive, and destructive. It hurt most as I remembered my daughter, who had been in the gifted program but was not able to finish high school. The children never learned from their mother or father how to deal with real life. My depression was fueled by never knowing what Bertha's next plot might cause.

2002

After being with Ted for nine years, he and I were finally able to make a journey to Cambodia. It was my first time to return home since I had escaped from there more than twenty years before.

After we landed in Phnom Penh, I was surprised to see how fast the economy in Cambodia had grown after everything was destroyed by the Khmer Rouge. Real estate was booming, and prices were going up. New construction was popping up everywhere, from the big city all the way out to the countryside, to the suburbs, and in between.

Everything looked so different from the way it looked before the war. People had flooded into the cities. Traffic was overwhelming with cars and motorcycles jammed together on the streets. It was not the calm, peaceful, and beautiful place I had known before. Many of the beautiful flowers and gardens had been trampled down and built over.

The weather in Cambodia is beautiful all year round and there are only three seasons, so there is no real need for winter coats. The land is rich, supporting an abundance of vegetables and minerals. The waters teem with all sorts of fish. Rich land attracted many foreigners to move to Cambodia. For me, however, wherever I went, my mind was so consumed with the absence of my children, not knowing if my children were safe or needed me, that I had no real time to think about the pain that came years before. Nonetheless, it was always in the background.

In 2001, there was a family at a local church who were missionaries in Phnom Penh. A couple of months after they arrived, we received a picture of their kids standing in front of a large house. It was my family's house, my home. There were some changes, like a new roof on top of what had been a rooftop deck and some sort of Sunsilk shampoo advertising banner hanging outside. But there was no doubt that this was the house I had lived in for most of my childhood. It was where I had a mom and a dad, brothers and sisters.

We had kept in touch with the church family, and they were kind enough to let us stay with them. After a few days in Phnom Penh, I was able to contact an old friend and classmate. She invited us to stay with her family, which was closer to the city center. Her brother and her husband were in the government and worked for Hun Sen, prime minister of Cambodia. It was from them that we were able to find out who the current "owners" of my parents' house were. When we were young, before the Khmer Rouge, my classmate, her brother, and my brothers all used to hang out together at our parents' house in Phnom Penh. They knew exactly where our house was, and she and her son took Ted and me to see it.

In 1979, soon after the Vietnamese took over the country, my siblings Rick, Thyda, and Charnay went to check our parents' house three times. On their first visit, a Vietnamese soldier guarded the gate and would not let them in. After the high-ranking Vietnamese officers left and the Cambodian military took over, they tried a second visit. The Cambodian military did not let them in either. On their third visit, the people who had moved into the house pointed a gun at them and threatened to kill them. My siblings finally gave up. I regretted so much that I was unable to go with them. As the eldest sibling, I knew more about everything our parents owned. By the time I was able to go, I wanted to check on not only the main house but also their former rental properties, located not far away from our main house. However, due to the new development and changes made to the houses, they were unrecognizable. What a broken heart! I regretted so much not being able to check on our plantation or our rice field. From what I understand, it was too dangerous to visit them without a guard.

We were surprised when a woman who said she was the sister of the owner invited us in to see the main house. Of course, all the old furniture was gone. With her and other people who were there to escort us, I did not have a chance to look under the staircase where we hid the silver items. I have a feeling all of the silver pieces we had hidden under the staircase were probably long gone as well. Also, several walls had been added; it had been carved up for multiple tenants. The second floor, as it turned out, had been leased to Unilever. This explained the Sunsilk shampoo banner outside. The house was large with three levels (four with the new roof), and there were three distinct sections from front to back. From what we could see in our short time there, at least eight families lived there, not counting the area leased to Unilever.

Every time I thought about our home, my heart would shatter as it reminded me of all of my parents' hard work. There were a lot of special memories in that house. I had hoped to buy back the family home. But as we talked more, the numbers wouldn't add up, partly from my rusty Khmer language skills, partly from the speed at which she was speaking, and partly from her local dialect. Because of the pleasant, beautiful weather all year round and the rich land, many foreigners—mainly Chinese, Japanese, and Korean—and businesspeople were attracted to the area and were willing to spend big money to invest in property. Property became extremely expensive, and the price kept going up over time.

The lady with whom we talked asked for several hundred thousand US dollars for just the front third of the house. That was more than the price that we paid for our house on the lake in South Carolina. We were stunned that we were not able to afford it. The woman had no patience for us once she knew we weren't ready to buy, and we were quickly asked to leave the property. I was heartbroken, and it felt as if my chest were being torn apart from the inside.

We headed back to my classmate's house and did not return. Later my classmate and her family took us to the southwest, to the small mountain called Phnom Kirirom. In my memory that place was a small part of paradise, surrounded by God's beautiful nature, filled with colorful flowers, cool streams of water flowing from giant rocks, and cool breezes flowing through giant trees. In my memory, time ceased when one was there, and one would wonder if the garden of Eden had been such a place.

Reality returned all too quickly. The land was so "naked" now. Almost all of the huge trees had been hacked down and shipped off to other countries. Entire hillsides near the mountain had been clear-cut and left bald. The cool breeze remained but now carried with it the dust from the road. The cool, running waters remained, the sound was still calming, and some younger trees remained, giving enough shade to still enjoy the music of the water. On the way up the mountain, and even at the top, there were numerous small sheds erected where people sold all sorts of food and other wares to the passersby.

We went on to the southern coastal town of Sihanoukville to enjoy the beach and the blue salty water, which were still the same. Next, we headed north to the city of Siem Reap to see the ruins of the great Angkor Wat. Each time we found "paradise" had been stripped away, like at Kirirom Mountain. The cool breezes carrying the perfume from rumduol wildflowers and wild fruit trees were gone. The majesty of the giant forests was all put asunder by man in the mad quest to dominate one over the other. Yes, the monuments still stood and were well taken care of, for there was the booming tourist trade to consider. It was no longer my land; it was no longer where I had grown up. Our home was no longer home. This too shall pass. My mind and my spirit will always be there for my family, even if I am not.

When I got back to the US, I checked with the Cambodian embassy in Washington, DC. There was no hope of getting anything back. Thanks to Google street maps, I've seen the place as it has changed over the years. The high metal fence along the street is gone now, and the front yard now has a roof over it. The Sunsilk shampoo banner is now gone, and it appears that the first floor (front section) and the front yard are being used as a restaurant.

Chapter 24

NOVICE INVESTOR

For the Lord *will vindicate his people*
and have compassion on his servants.

—Psalm 135:14

2007

My journey continued after a powerful earthly lesson. This continuous thunderstorm of turmoil wiped out everything I had and left nothing. I surrendered all, and it became a wake-up call. I felt as if I came out from a long tunnel. I needed to do something more productive that would provide security for my Alex and Mony and our next generation. Now the world was so open to me. This destruction allowed me to search for the lost love and affection of my children. As I promised my parents I'd be strong, it hurt when I let my children down. I desperately wanted to give them back something tangible for our future generation. To battle with this earth for my loved ones, I needed new strength to move forward. God gave me the ability to move mountains. I began to discover my own identity and my own true soul and to be connected to God, the Supernatural Being that saved my life and brought me closer to my children.

My intention is to be who I am. William Ernest Henley wrote, "I am the master of my fate; I am the captain of my soul." I am associated with the source of all that is possible. Through my Creator and through His glory, anything is possible for me. I am a child of God, a spiritual human being, with a soul that gives me the potential to fulfill my dreams. My faith is the rock that sustained me when I got in step with my God, who gave me a unique gift that I can offer to this planet. It is a miracle of grace that He allowed me to step into something bigger than I can imagine. Bertha and the Khmer Rouge wiped out everything I used to have, but God replaced it.

I decided to start investing in properties so I could have something tangible to pass on to my children before I died, even though I had no money, no experience, and no one to help me figure it out.

I received several loans from a couple of banks who held mortgages on my properties. We lived hand-to-mouth for a while as I was determined to pay off my loans as soon as possible. And I did pay them back, but it took a long time. This was an incredibly stressful time in my life. I used to have nightmares about being broke.

Ted always supported me, in his own way. No matter how much we lost, he would put in more time at his job. He couldn't face ordeals head-on, so all the decisions were mine alone, and I had to be responsible for them, which put more burden on me.

In addition to the money issues that come with real estate, we also had to deal with crooks, shady contractors, and ongoing bad tenants. But, God also sent me some good handymen who taught me how to do things, and I tried hard to learn from them so I could save money and understand more about that part of the business. They showed me how to do upkeep on small things.

But my pathway to becoming a businesswoman was strewn with roadblocks. In the first few years, there were huge struggles and a large amount of money lost to crooked contractors. They took advantage of a fledgling like me. I ended up with huge debts that I wasn't sure we were ever going to pay off.

I felt as if I'd jumped into a frying pan. I didn't realize how difficult the real estate rental business was. I was basically going it alone, managing all sixteen rentals by myself. It was extremely stressful. Among my sixteen rental properties, there was always something that needed my attention. In addition to payments on several loans, high taxes, high insurance, and miscellaneous repairs, there is always an ongoing issue with a destructive tenant who doesn't pay their rent and damages our properties. Among sixteen rentals, there are three who stand out as by far the worst. These happened at different times, but each was devastating.

Lord, how many are my foes!
How many rise up against me!
—Psalm 3:1

The first one was a crooked contractor who brainwashed me and told me that he was going to remodel the building. He took $67,000 cash. The building originally was in good shape; it just needed painting and small touch-ups. Instead, he demolished the building from the roof to the foundation. We had to hire another licensed contractor, which cost us an additional $125,000, to rebuild what the first one destroyed. This happened my first year of running the business.

A few years later the second one happened. A tenant turned our house into an unlicensed group home without telling me. The contract stated it was to be occupied by five people; our neighbor told me they saw at least eighteen to twenty people residing on our property. The house was not ADA compliant or set up for a group home. All of her people received government checks and needed shelter. She made holes in all the kitchen cabinets and refrigerator doors to install padlocks for everyone to store their food. There were several old leaky, rusty refrigerators and several flimsy cots in every room. Bedbugs were everywhere. Ambulances showed up every day and broke our driveway. She collected money for these "services" while she literally destroyed and vandalized our property and didn't pay her final month's rent. She left behind several months of unpaid water bills, so we couldn't turn the water back on to do the repairs until we paid her final bill. In the two years she was there, she left extensive repairs throughout the entire house, including needing to rebuild all three bathrooms, replace all the appliances, and make all the other general repairs after her people moved out. It cost us $67,000, in addition to the jobs several helpers and I did to keep costs down. I consequently injured myself during those repairs to bring the buildings back to a livable condition.

The third one we found out a few years later, after the pandemic. Over the course of their five-year stay, the tenant used our property for a pet-sitting business without authorization and without paying any pet fee. Those three tenants vandalized and left our properties in such a state that they went beyond what could be repaired by any handyman. Unfortunately, insurance refused to pay on these three major repair projects. I had to hire licensed contractors to rebuild and repair in order to make these properties livable again. These three drained me financially and emotionally. It was an extremely difficult time, as bad as Bertha and worse than the Khmer Rouge. I cried to God for redemption to compensate my loss and grant me peace to move forward. It was enough to kill me; I let God take charge.

Unfortunately, having a business without a strong support person by my side was a true struggle, both financially and emotionally draining, which put more stress on Ted's and my relationship. I became more aware of the bad things happening around me. I felt as though I had definitely brought myself into a deeper pit.

Ted retired from the computer chip company at the age of fifty-eight. He received fifteen months of severance pay and used a part of his 401(k) to pay leftover balances on two smaller loans and to pay for the major repairs on our property, especially the damage done by the woman who used my house for a group home.

More stresses piled up on top of me, one after another, with pressure all the time. Fear of losing your home is more than anyone ever wants to face. Long story short, it took me several years just to get my head above water. Thank God who blessed me with good tenants to overcome the ongoing bad tenants. Later, I learned to deal with many roadblocks, crooks, and bad tenants. These ordeals must have been sent from God to test me. He helped me and my children all the way. We became stronger.

When Bertha found out that I owned several properties, she wanted part of them. She found a way to get in touch with Mony and Alex through Facebook and convinced them to contact me. So, one day, out of the blue, after not hearing from them for several years, I got a surprise call from my children, asking me to split property with Ted. I later found out that Bertha had put them up to it. She went through my children to get to our properties and gossip about us by telling me how bad my Mony talked about me. Ted and I talked about this latest predicament, and we decided to have an attorney set up our trust, with some assets going to the children and some donated to the church and community services.

* * *

I will build you up again,
and you, Virgin Israel, will be rebuilt.
Again you will take up your timbrels
and go out to dance with the joyful.

—Jeremiah 31:4

My first year after a big loss from a crook, the real estate market started to crash, and there were so many foreclosure properties popping up everywhere. God was by my side, and He gave me strength to keep going. This became an opportunity for me to purchase more properties under market price. In 2013, I ended up owning and having occupants in sixteen properties. It was a challenging business, collecting every penny from renters to pay off loans and high property taxes and to maintain the properties.

After all these challenges, I am grateful that our Supernatural God has blessed and is blessing our lives. In the midst of trials and in my land of suffering, He continues to sanctify us through my investment business, and He also blessed my children. God delivers those whom He loves from wickedness and the deceitful spirit.

With God's help, I turned my wounds, failures, and mistakes into a sort of wisdom. My secret to success was God who rules over my life, and I allowed myself to be attached to God, who overheard me. And in His righteousness, He rescued me and vindicated me.

It took a lonely woman like me several years and a great deal of effort to run this type of business. I am not sure how I was able to come this far without someone emotionally strong to stand by my side. Ted is not emotionally strong, but at least he stayed by my side.

My intention is to fulfill the dream my highest Creator is calling me to fulfill. I am in charge of my own destiny. I am the master of my own fate, my own soul, my own glories. I allow my real me to come through, and I listen to my own intuition. I am responsible for my own life before God.

I am who I am. I follow my God. He gives me the ability to rise above all my suffering.

I was sustained by the power of love and attachment for my family. I survived losing the ability to help my children and to protect my next generation, who had been through what I had been through. I was saved by God. He gave me the strength to move mountains.

I pray that my legacy is love, compassion, honesty, truth, and forgiveness. Whatever happened between me and my children, they are still my blood, and, as a mother, I intend to protect them and the next generation and to empower those who have gone through what I have gone through. God's grace allowed me to be a successful entrepreneur.

When I look back, I ask myself how many people would be able to run this type of complex business without either a strong family member to support them or a strong partner who has knowledge and the ability to deal with this world, which is filled with so many opportunistic crooks. This type of business is extremely challenging for a lonely Asian woman and an introverted husband. This must have been from God, who performed another miracle in my life.

> *Then the* LORD *your God will restore your fortunes . . . and gather you again from all the nations where he scattered you.*
>
> —Deuteronomy 30:3

God is always by my side. In 2020–22, after the COVID-19 pandemic, the real estate market went up and I was able to sell five properties (including one of the last and worst ones that was used for pet sitting) to pay off the rest of the mortgages. What a miracle. God is a living God.

It took me more than ten years to get my business this far. It was difficult and incredibly stressful. I couldn't have had the strength to prevail on my own. It was with the help of God that I got through the burden of loss after loss.

I was in need at one point in my life. Now I am grateful to give back to His people through community services. I am slowly gaining freedom from countless strains and distress. I am now able to take some time off to focus, relax, and celebrate my success. Now I am financially free and own a successful business. Both Alex and Mony are also doing exceedingly well. People who used to reject me now tell me how well I've done. I said that I am a lost sheep; I can't do it without God. Thanks be to God!

Chapter 25

CHILDREN AND THEIR LOVED ONES RETURN

2011

Every night I used to close my eyes and wonder how my children were doing. One night in 2011, I had a vivid dream. In it, there were voices calling someone Joseph and another name, Jacob. I was told he would be a blessing to us. At first, I wasn't sure what that meant, but my dream seemed very clear when I woke up. Sure enough, later I heard from my daughter that she was expecting.

We found out that she was going to have a son, and she decided to name him Timothy Joseph. It was amazing how accurate my dream was. Yes, God answered my prayers. He knew how vulnerable I was, worrying about my Mony's safety. I was excited for a long time. I wish that I could have been in Los Angeles when my grandson was born. I wish I could have babysat my grandson whom God granted to us.

The relationship between my daughter and me was still strained, however, so I tried to give her the space she asked for. I wish I could have been there to support my daughter when my grandson came into our lives. But my burning anxieties subsided when I found out his father is a mature, smart, gentle, caring, generous, and loving man who has an incredibly successful career, especially for such a young age. We are all incredibly happy. God has shone his light upon us through my grandson. What a magnificent, precious gift from God.

At the same time, I occupied myself by dealing with my business dilemmas. When I look back on those days, I wonder where I was getting all the strength to fight on so many fronts and am surprised by how much I have accomplished thus far.

A few years ago, when my grandson was only three years old, I told him that when he grows older and stronger, I wanted to teach him a headstand pose. He said to me, "You show me first." The kid is very smart, just like his mommy and daddy.

I wanted to move closer to my daughter and be able to support her getting married. But real estate in Los Angeles, especially in Beverly Hills, is beyond what we could afford. Even selling all of my properties in South Carolina wouldn't have allowed me to buy a small empty lot.

Even so, I am grateful my grandson has the opportunity to grow up there. As a small-business owner with many responsibilities, I can't just drop everything and leave. All I can do is continue to pray to God for a miracle that would enable us to become closer to each other spiritually and physically, with joy and hope.

August 2012

Ultimately, I got caught during a business dilemma, when my children brought their loved ones to spend time with me. It was five years after I started a business when things got worse—perhaps the most stressful time in my entire life and it just happened to coincide with a visit from both Alex and Mony to introduce their loved ones to me. Mony was bringing my ten-month-old grandson and his father. Alex was bringing his girlfriend to spend time with us. This should have been a most blessed time for me. Finally, after so many years of praying for this very day to come, my beloved children and their loved ones were coming home to me. It should have been the happiest moment of my entire life. Instead, it was disastrous, and it would be the longest time before we were together again. Oh, Lord my God, please heal our broken hearts!

At first I was so excited to see my Alex and my Mony, whom I missed so much. I wanted so much to carry my grandson in my arms, but having tremendous back pain prevented me from carrying him and holding him closer to my heart. I also wanted to kiss and wrap my arms around my future son- and daughter-in-law. But, something in my brain went wrong, and the hell of darkness broke loose. It seemed like my hope evaporated in the sun. A wave of the unthinkable washed over me from the deepest distraction and most recent emotional pain. I did not understand why I allowed this dark energy to affect us again. I must have been overwhelmed with stress from my back injury, from my business dilemma, from a recently purchased home on a big lake, from the subsequent move to that home, from preparing for the children's visit, and from preparing a large party to introduce my friends from our church to my family. I also foolishly asked Bertha to help me cook for that party because I had no one else to help me. All she did was hound Ted and me to try to sell all of our properties. She also wanted us to write our wills with her as the beneficiary. She was relentless. It must have been all too much at one time.

Hear my cry for help,
my King and my God,
for to you I pray.
In the morning, LORD, you hear my voice;
in the morning I lay my requests before you
and wait expectantly.

—Psalm 5:2–3

Oh, God, please help me and protect us from any harm. Something went wrong again! How exhausted I was. The same sort of dark energy completely blocked me and caused me to lose my true identity again—the same thing that happened the last time my children left me. I was alone again. Just like I was alone after the Khmer Rouge, but this time I had a sick husband and a sick brother. I think my brain must have been in some state of shock or exhaustion. I felt as though there was a dark wall blocking me from thinking clearly; I was unable to have open communications with my children and their loved ones. Instead, I manifested caustic anger and frustration toward them and their friends who came to visit them. The whole world around us turned upside down. Here again my actions were the mistake of a lifetime. It wasn't toward just Alex and Mony this time; I manifested it toward my future son- and daughter-in-law. I never again saw them all together. How hateful a mother I was toward my children. Deep in my heart, I needed them more than anything else on this earth; nevertheless, I regretted not being able to embrace them. Instead, I unintentionally pushed them and their loved ones further away from me. What a monster I was toward them. It was not the real me. Without understanding this, my children have a right to hate me. Yes, I admitted I was too toxic to be around the people whom I love more than anything else on this earth. What a painful memory.

After everyone left, I ended up weeping with my own bitterness in a vast empty space alone again. What mother on earth does not love her children? Since that time, the relationship with my children was never the same. I shuddered and wept to God for help to bring us back, to restore our relationship. I earnestly prayed that God would soften Alex and Mony's hearts to forgive me and to open communication with me again. I love to hear their voices. Without them there was a hole inside my soul, and only my children, my grandson, and their loved ones could fill it. Today and every day, I long for a full understanding and restoration in all of our lives.

How could I live without my children, my parents, my siblings, or any relatives? I felt so hopeless. I desperately wanted to take good care of my children, but I was depleted in mind, body, and spirit. My heartbreak magnified my sorrow. It was even worse than my memories of the Khmer Rouge. It was also oddly parallel to the time when my mother died. Every day since they left me, without hearing their voices, my heart shuddered and I wept alone, waiting for their return until exhaustion would overtake me. This went on for several years from the time I opened my eyes till the time I fell asleep

God is the only one who knows what is missing in my heart. With God's help from now on I promise to prepare myself, to not allow darkness to conquer us again. I am asking that my children and their loved ones—based on my own experiences with my mother-in-law—no longer be subjected to anything like that. From now on, I will do my best to be the best mother on earth to them. What a shameful and painful memory we've been through. I ask my Alex and Mony and my grandson's father to please forgive me and please give me a second chance.

> *"I am with you and will save you,"*
> *declares the* L*ORD.*
>
> —Jeremiah 30:11

The heavy storm was gone; the sky was clear. It must have been a miracle again. God is with us in every step of the way. I managed to pay off loans, and my business is doing much better in the past sixteen years. I have financial freedom to hire more than one property management company to take over my business. This will help free me from stresses. I'll be able to relax, to take a vacation, to enjoy fresh air, to sleep better, to think better. I am stronger. I am fully in charge. I ask everyone to have no more fear; I will no longer be who I was. With God's help, as long as I'm still alive, I will do my very best to protect us and no longer allow any dark spirit to interfere with the relationship between me and my loved ones ever again. With grace, God grants me the ability and assets to protect my next generation. More than anything in my entire life I need you, my children and my grandchildren.

I want us back as a functional normal loving family again.

* * *

My brother David moved closer to the Khmer community in Lowell, Massachusetts, a few years after we got to the US. In 2010, a few years after I started my business, we moved him back to stay with us so I could take care of him.

God gave me the strength and compassion to care for David and the ability to be a blessing to the rest of my family.

Even though my children have many reasons to hate me, I asked them both to forgive me. I prayed that the Lord would open the door for us and would prevent the dark force from interfering with us. I asked them to work with me and to stay strong when I can't assist them. I asked them to give me a chance to calm down and be patient. I was just awakening from the stresses of existing in a constant state of survival. All I wanted was to have us back together as a family. I wished to see both of my children get married and start their own families. And I wanted to see them build their faith in God.

No matter what happens in life, I pray that God will change our hearts so that we become better people—more loving, compassionate, forgiving, and supportive of one another. I pray God grants me the chance to see everyone accept me for who I am, and not how I reacted when I was traumatized.

I wished to spend more time with my children. But because we were dealing with so much stress, it was hard when we saw one another. In the past, we ended up getting into fights that pushed us further apart and we were unable to communicate for several years; but as time passed, I changed, and we no longer fought as we did before.

I will never leave you nor forsake you.

—Hebrews 13:5 ESV

2013

In addition to my desire to be reunited with my children, I desperately wanted to reunite with my sister Thyda. In 2013, we visited Thyda in Australia, after she came to see me here in the US. I did my best to accommodate her when she came here. During our visit to her in Australia, one evening, while having dinner at her house, I was shocked when Thyda's son asked me why I hadn't taken his mother to the US with me. I was heartbroken; it was very hard to explain to him, as it involved his mother's fight with me. Thyda stood there and did not say a word.

Earlier, I had asked Thyda's daughter to visit us anytime, as she worked in New York City. I told her that I would be glad to pay for the ticket and whatever else she needed help with, for her to come and visit us and to stay at our home as long as she wished. Now that I was financially successful in the US, as an entrepreneur, I wished for Thyda's children to keep in touch with me and my children. We are all family. I wanted them to grow closer together. I learned from my first trip there that Thyda still carried bad feelings that might have kept this from happening.

If I ever visit Australia again, I will travel with a group and have my own place to stay. There would be less stress for both me and Thyda. Although life is still upside down sometimes, I still love my family very much and wish that one day, with God's help, I will be able to reach out to all of my siblings and their children (as long as they are willing to accept me). Ultimately, there is nothing I can do to change Thyda's feelings about me, no more than I can change the past.

I earnestly pray to God to open everyone's hearts in our family: children, brothers, sisters, and their children. I pray for healing and understanding. Lastly, I pray that God will give me the strength and ability to reach out to everyone's heart before it's too late.

* * *

I am so pleased to know that my children are both physically and financially independent and have done so well without us. My daughter became an actress and a manager for an electric car company in Los Angeles. With support from my grandson's father, she has purchased an expensive home in the LA area. She is a good mother to my grandson. I am proud of the woman she has become.

Mony and her son are in good, strong hands as my grandson's father takes good care of both of them. He has provided them a safe and healthy environment.

My son became a financial analyst and a manager for a company in Washington, DC. He survived the holocaust of Cambodia, the loss of his father, and near starvation by sucking baby corn juice. After college he left home to teach in some very cold places overseas. He managed to pay his way through university and recently purchased a second house in a historical area. He accomplished so many things on his own. I am enormously proud of him.

Our righteous God is watching over us. Everything comes from His great love, and we have done exceedingly well. I am thankful to know that God never goes silent, nor does fear control Him. He has never left us. He has never forsaken us. He continues to heal us. Thanks be to God.

Chapter 26

LEGACY AND REFLECTION

"He who scattered Israel will gather them
and will watch over his flock like a shepherd."

. . . .

They will be like a well-watered garden,
and they will sorrow no more.

—Jeremiah 31:10, 12

As I get older, the time has come for me to prepare to leave my legacy and to prepare for my eventual death. Starting my own business and investing in real estate allowed me to have tangible assets to pass on to the next generation and to donate to community charities so that I can die in peace and with a good conscience. Charnay was a bit cynical of my idea. She reminded me how our parents invested all they had in their properties, but their children never benefited from their hard work. Of course I worried from time to time that the same could happen to me and my children. I would feel hopeless and assume that things would remain as they are, but there is no major communist power here. I saw that the United States was not Cambodia and that here, my plans just might work out as long as I pay my property tax and all bills on time and continue to maintain my properties. I think they are going to be okay.

My persistence in following this idea through had to do with how bad I had been as a mother. I did try, to the best of my ability, to be there for my children and to take care of them, but I always fell short in my efforts. This business idea was a chance for me to redeem myself. Well, it would not get me complete redemption, but I wanted to make life easier for my children.

Then you will call, and the LORD will answer;
you will cry for help, and he will say: Here am I.

—Isaiah 58:9

"and heal your wounds,"

. . . .

and have compassion on his dwellings;
the city will be rebuilt on her ruins,
and the palace will stand in its proper place.

. . . .

and the sound of rejoicing.
I will add to their numbers,

. . . .

"So you will be my people,
and I will be your God."

—Jeremiah 30:17–22

As a result of that hard work and persistence, I'm now financially able to support my family and relatives, which is something I couldn't have done only a few years ago. Everything I own will pass on to my children and our next generation. My possessions will go to those I love. I also want part of my handiwork to be offered back to God through His community with love.

My children now live far away from me. They have their own lives and show no interest in moving back to South Carolina. But, this happens to many of us as our children grow up and make their own way. Even though they are not physically close to me, I appreciate seeing them doing well and being accepted. I do get nervous for them from time to time, but I have to put all in God's hands and leave Him in charge. I am focusing on one day at a time and striving for peace. The key to peace is to understand the mind and heart. Our mental state is based on how we view the world we live in. We have to rely on our faith in God to guide our travels through life.

In 2018, Ted was diagnosed with Parkinson's disease, and it has progressed somewhat. That progression has made me even more determined. When real estate prices went up, we sold a couple of our properties to pay off mortgages and loans and make home improvements. With Ted's health declining and both of us aging, I've now hired more than one management company to take care of all our local long-term rentals and our vacation rentals at the beach. In June 2022, I purchased a vacation home at Pawleys Island, which is a few minutes' walk to the beach and has a golf course in the backyard.

We have so much to be thankful for. And we can offer back to our divine God who is always with me and my children. After all the times we hit rock bottom in our lives, God brought us back up. Without the Lord, I am not sure how we would have survived.

* * *

The Khmer Rouge, Bertha, business dilemmas, and ongoing issues with bad tenants—it was all challenging and brought indescribable sorrow, pain, defeat, and loss. But, there was a reason God helped me live through my business problems and saved my life those three times during the Khmer Rouge regime. It was a challenge for my soul. Because I am human like everyone else, I was blind, deaf, mute, hurt, selfish, and greedy. My guilt was so great and I was lacking the capacity to love as much as I should have. Because of that and my unwillingness to serve, my sins blinded me and increased my suffering.

I am sorry for my past with everything that happened. I thought I did my best, but I had lost the ability to stand up and take care of everyone's needs, including those of my own children. I've often felt that I am still numb and unable to recover from those losses. I still have a lot of vulnerability when it comes to my family and children, even after forty years. But we all have to find our way out of this pit and let our anger go. It is our fate.

I asked God to restore the relationship among me, my children, my grandson, and their loved ones, and also to rescue me from loneliness and darkness. I asked for forgiveness to change me into the person He wanted me to be. I fought, holding on to my faith, for as long as I could, and God gave me new strength. I stood up on my own feet once again and came face-to-face with the destruction Bertha had caused us throughout the years and later with all the business predicaments. Even though my children had moved away, I never gave up believing that I could mend my relationship with them. I woke up each day ready to face whatever life had to throw at me. Life is unfair. There is just so much destruction in the world, and I have experienced more than my fair share. But, ultimately, God fights on my behalf.

At the same time, I am crying for justice for those who died unjustly during the war. I am praying for peace on this earth and healing among us, including my brothers and sisters.

* * *

I genuinely believe that we are all human beings born with the propensity to sin, lost in darkness and transgressions, drawn into temptation, which I fear is not easy to abstain from. Life has a divine purpose that we need to associate with our soul. We all are seeking light to shine on us, and Jesus is that light. We will be rewarded if we abstain from doing wrong, from wickedness, and from immoral acts.

Jesus said in Psalm 4:4–5:

> Tremble and do not sin;
>   when you are on your beds,
>   search your hearts and be silent.
> Offer the sacrifices of the righteous
>   and trust in the Lord.

Jesus is the Light that has led me to repentance and forgiveness. I try to imprint His words on my heart. Through Him, anything is possible.

Forgiveness

God is our vindicator, and the Lord is a God of justice. Give all your suffering and burning to Him. God has restored everything I lost, giving me a double portion better than what I lost (Deuteronomy 30:3–13).

Being able to forgive provides true healing for my soul. I surrendered to God, asked for help to let go of anger, pain, and loss, and gave them all to Him. This freed me to act not from my sinful nature and gave my soul peace and serenity. One day when I leave this earth, I will stand in front of the Judge with a clean heart and pure soul.

We are told to forgive and forget, but this is not always easy. Unforgiveness leads to anger and outrage, but after I reached the level where I was able to let go, it freed my soul, healed my heart, and set my soul free from the prison of darkness. When I reached that point, I become a better person with no more bitterness, free of pain, without need for revenge or grudges, and no more a prisoner of my own past mistakes. I am at peace, totally free to be able to receive the gifts that God has for me.

Serving

Jesus came to serve, not to be served.

I have learned that when I offer my time and service to those who need help, I experience healing. I am trying to be more productive, more willing to serve and to give of myself, and more helpful to others. This is the most effective way to honor myself—by serving others, whether rich or poor, professional or non-skilled, anyone who is in need. My legacy will be determined by my service to others.

Now that I have more time, I am so grateful that I am able to serve through volunteering. Anything that I can do to serve is my privilege. I am giving my own time and effort, offering back to my God who gave me success. God will heal my broken heart with vision, perception, and understanding because I know that there is someone greater than me in charge of my life who is as steady as a rock.

Doing Good Deeds

I believe in doing good deeds and doing the right thing no matter where you are or what the circumstances are. I know that if I do things wrong it will sooner or later come back and haunt me. My hope is that I maintain morality, dignity, honesty, and integrity all the time, as long as I live. I believe that our highest Divine Spirit, who lives inside of us, is watching everything we do. This world may not recognize me for it, but my Highest Divine inside of me will bless and protect me and grant me great rewards.

It took me years to stand up on my own feet and set up boundaries. This allows me to be connected to the power that rules over my life and to connect with my sacred Being that is greater than me, that higher power called God, and to allow Him to instruct me. Through His supreme power, anything is possible.

I will never give up on believing that there is a supreme, all-powerful Being watching over me and over every one of us. God is inside of all of us; that is why we all know what is right and what is wrong. I see it in many ways. He saved me and my children many times, but I was as blinded as anyone else, and we all got caught up in many earthly things and forgot who watched over us.

Meditation

Meditation is my daily practice, usually before I fall asleep and after I get up from bed. I normally spend a few minutes praying and talking to God and expressing all of the concerns I have for that day, by surrendering, submerging, and giving all burdens to Him. The most effective one for me is either through reading or listening to the Bible. God's Word is very powerful when I turn my attention inward to listen to my heart and purify my mind. But, there are several kinds of meditation. When I am grounded with His wisdom, grace, and faith, especially when I am lost in the darkness of despair from my past experiences, God will find me and grant me the strength and courage to come back home each and every time. My creator has pulled me back from my long, dark battle of many years.

It only takes a few minutes each time to tune myself inward, to tune my mind to the center of my heart, and to embrace myself at the present moment either walking, sitting, standing, or lying. I take deep breaths anywhere, anyplace I can think to do it. Knowing I am God's child, I start to bring myself to my inmost secret thoughts. Then I seal His commands in my heart. Each and every time I feel bad, I ask God for help to refrain from negative thoughts, holding nothing against anyone. Life is a trial, and everything on earth is temporary. I let go and forgive those who hurt me, knowing God is in charge. It is very powerful how I have come this far after more than forty-five years of suffering. Our minds are continually active, like a monkey jumping here and there, bouncing around left and right every second. When I start to doubt, I go back to my center, again and again, finding my happiness in the small moments now, not tomorrow or yesterday, no judging, having no expectations. I give up things that do not belong to me, focus on love, move on with grace, and do no harm to others. I change this moment to something better and greater. I appreciate what is now, and that connects me to my God. I listen to my heart at this very moment, and it helps me cope with daily life. This is grounding me to be more mindful, draws me closer to the heavenly spirit, and gives me the wisdom to be kind. By doing these things, I free myself to accomplish more good things.

I try to self-correct every step of the way to turn myself into a better person. Life has taught me an important lesson: never stop believing.

Chapter 27

THE PROMISED LAND

Instead of your shame
you will receive a double portion. . . .
"For I, the Lord, love justice;
I hate robbery and wrongdoing. . . .
All who see them will acknowledge
that they are a people the Lord has blessed. . . .
For he has clothed me with garments of salvation.

—Isaiah 61:7–10

From our hard labor endeavor, we now rejoice in gathering and harvesting our success that our God has granted us along with many freedoms. Loans are paid off, and we are now able to be free from most stress and to relax and to sleep better. We've opened the door to accept our loved ones and whoever is willing to return, be it children, grandchildren, family, friends, or relatives, near and far.

I plead that our Lord will continue to strengthen and open everyone's heart, healing and drawing us back to one another. As I get older, I am looking forward to enjoying the last part of my life around my children and grandchildren. I want to spend precious time together, enjoy sunshine and fresh air, free from troubles, free from old wounds, and no longer dealing with obstacles. I'm so ready for my retirement to start and to spend more time on volunteer work. As I said, during the midst of prosecution, God blessed me and my children in many miraculous ways. I truly believe in my supernatural heavenly eternity. I am doing great. Thanks be to God.

God is our ultimate answer. He provides redemption and vindication for His people. Talk to God, give Him all your burdens, and let Him be in charge. He will compensate your loss.

> *Be strong in the Lord and in his mighty power. Put on the full armor of God, so that you can take your stand against the devil's schemes.*
>
> —Ephesians 6:10–11

I want to pass my great experiences and my understanding on to my children and to the next generation and to urge them to align themselves with God and hold His doctrines in their hearts. I know that then success will follow. Through Him, all things are possible.

> *Yet a time is coming and has now come when the true worshipers will worship the Father in the Spirit and*

in truth, for they are the kind of worshipers the Father seeks. God is spirit, and his worshipers must worship in the Spirit and in truth.

—John 4:23–24

I've learned to practice harmony and to serve others who need help. I found out that God's instructions are exceedingly powerful, so I have stamped them on my heart. If we are able to align ourselves with these holy rules, then success and peace will follow.

Life is a true testimonial, a trial, a battle between God and evil. I wish to pass my experiences to everyone.

Strengthening the disciples and encouraging them to remain true to the faith. "We must go through many hardships to enter the kingdom of God."

—Acts 14:22

Rules to Cultivate Success

[God] set all the boundaries of the earth.

—Psalm 74:17

I am the L*ORD your God,*
who teaches you what is best for you.

—Isaiah 48:17

My son, do not forget my teaching,
but keep my commands in your heart,

for they will prolong your life many years
and bring you peace and prosperity.
Let love and faithfulness never leave you;
bind them around your neck,
write them on the tablet of your heart.
. . . .
Trust in the LORD *with all your heart*
. . . .
fear the LORD *and shun evil.*

—Proverbs 3:1–3, 5, 7

These are daily rules that I practice to cultivate peace and success:

1. Practice love, compassion, and forgiveness.
2. Do not lie, steal, or kill.
3. Do not be involved in sexual immorality.
4. Surrender to God, accepting His will.
5. Donate generously to the poor.
6. Serve others and those who need help.
7. Meditate on God's Word, purifying your mind.
8. Be honest, dignified, with morality and integrity.
9. Turn away from sin. Do what is right.
10. Build trust. Do not judge. Avoid intoxication.

I am human, not perfect. All I can do is repent, turn myself to God, and do my best to honor these universal rules. Although, it is not easy; it requires a lot of patience, hardship, persevering, and faith. Deep in my heart, life is doing what is right and just and fair (Proverbs 1:3), therefore I asked God to give me more strength to keep going. I aligned myself with God's law and am doing my best to strive much harder to battle this earth.

Life is a trial. Everything on earth is temporary. Therefore, we want our hearts to be clean to prepare ourselves to leave this earth, especially when we stand in front of the Judge. We definitely want to leave this earth with a clean heart and a clear conscience.

I wish to pass this practice on to my children and our next generation. I have found that the rules of success are aligned with universal law, and that one of them, not lying, is almost universal in nature. We all tend to classify lies as significant or insignificant. This is to say that circumstances determine what is dignity, honesty, and morality. If it does no harm, why is it sin? Sin is sin. Avoid sin.

Jesus said to love God, love one another, forgive, have compassion, love your neighbor as you love yourself, and help the poor, the orphans, and the widows. We should want to help those less fortunate. Remember, every good deed we offer to God is planting a seed that grows into something that helps our soul and spirit. Good deeds cleanse our hearts and please the heavenly Father.

These scriptures are God's commands in the Christian Holy Bible and in every ethical manual ever given for human life. I have faith that they are especially important to every culture and every religion. We all live under these rules, and we all are aware of these laws. Therefore, no matter what happens, I honor them, and I try my best to obey them. The temptation to sin is so powerful that sometimes it is not easy to stay fearful all the time. We are all human and born with the propensity to sin. Ultimately, each of us will make our own choice to either do good or do evil.

John 14:6 says, "Jesus said . . ., I am the way, and the truth, and the life; no one comes to the Father but through Me" (NASB 1995).

The Bible states that the way to heaven is very narrow, because we must go through many hardships to enter the kingdom of God, and the path to hell is much wider. Because it is easy to fall into temptation, to live without morality, it is easy to fall into a life of sin as it is more fun than living with dignity and morality. However, if we accept our sufferings and accept God in our hearts and are willing to follow His will, accept our responsibilities, and have faith in God who sent His son to die for our sins, He will help us on earth. We already have a home in heaven awaiting us. One day we will enter heaven's door.

Thank God for helping us come this far. From time to time, I had given up hope, being ridden with guilt and fear. But as I watch YouTube regarding the gospel, listen to God and Jesus Christ, and read my Bible and meditate on God's words, my life is changing and calming my soul. I give thanks to God.

Conclusion

LIGHT WILL SHINE, VICTORY WILL COME

Blessed is the man who fears the Lord,
who greatly delights in his commandments!

—Psalm 112:1 ESV

We are humans who reside in a confused world where no one is perfect. Sometimes we feel close to ourselves, and sometimes we feel a thousand miles away from our true self, lost in darkness, like lost sheep. Wherever we are lost, God always finds us. And every time we fail, He picks us up and, with grace, puts us back where we belong.

Through these years I survived through grace with a fresh, new spirit, I've been delivered from my sin into wisdom and peace. Every door will open to truth. Every storm will pass. Light will shine; victory will come.

We are all children of God. We all have angels and divine spirits guarding us, which emboldens us to be who we are. Through God, we have the power to develop our own personality and to control our minds and our thoughts, feeding our soul with integrity and love.

My long journey has taught me to be a better person. I have learned to develop and prepare myself to become more spiritually mature. Each day I train my mind to reflect on my past and to keep track in my journal of what I have done good for that day. To be really humble, we should concentrate on improving ourselves with good moral habits. We must place emphasis on self-development, encouraging ourselves to do good things and to become better people. The saying is, "Walk the good walk and talk the good talk." I try to do this as much as I can, although from time to time, the influences of this confusing world make occasional failures unavoidable. Of course, since followers of Jesus have the Holy Spirit living inside of us, we are able to know right from wrong. We see reality, and we have the ability to control our thoughts and emotions. Our thoughts are very powerful and can either build us up or tear us down. To control our thoughts, we must build up our intimate relationship with God.

I refuse to give up. I continue to do good things to the people around me and to myself. I try to follow the Divine laws and treat everyone as equals. I know this will be a positive in their lives and mine, and our God will be better served. Money will not save us; only God can save us. Earthly possessions impress people. We are visible to everyone's eyes when we have a good job and money. However, very few of us accept those who are poor; they are rejected in this world. In the end, God is the only one who can judge us for who we are and what is in our hearts.

Where there once was a hole in my heart, hope now fills every space. God is faithful to his people. The proof of that is that my personal relationships are improving. Because it was so painful, I haven't communicated with Bertha for several years, so I have no way to know if she has changed. All I can do is continue to encourage Ted to be open to his mother and his family. I am willing to support him. I always will love Thyda and her children, and I will do my best to embrace everyone as long as they are willing to accept me. We are family.

I haven't reunited with all of my siblings, who are now in France and Australia, in nearly forty years, but thanks to technology such as YouTube, Facebook Messenger, and WhatsApp, I can more easily reconnect with my family—both near and overseas. Happily, I have found out that they all are doing well; it gives me immense joy to hear this good news. My siblings' children have graduated from college. They have professional jobs and a better lifestyle.

I have shared my journey from tragedy to triumph so that you, dear reader, might be encouraged in your own faith journey. I must fulfill what I was called to do; thus, I was not surprised to hear the same request several times from many different people over a period of years that I write my story. They seemed to see something in me that I couldn't see for myself, but I refused to do it every time because the memories were just too painful. That was until my close friend told me I needed to put my stories in a book. My neighbor dentist even asked me why I didn't just sell my properties and write a book when he saw me in so much distress. At the time, I was battling with the tenant who turned my house into a group home. Not long before that, several of my other friends asked me the same question. One said I should write the bits and pieces down on paper each time I remembered, and I did. Suddenly the advice from the dentist and my friends combined to stir my heart and open my eyes. They were right; I felt like I was in so much pain struggling at the bottom of a pit with business dilemmas; I finally agreed with them. All of a sudden it sparked a light inside of my hopeless feelings. I decided it was time to write my story. So, here I am, sharing my troubles, losses, accomplishments, and victories.

Though I have suffered much, the Lord has advocated for me. I have been running my business now for sixteen years. My company is doing really well. The real estate market is getting hot. I am blessed with two kids and a wonderful grandson who are all doing extremely well financially and spiritually.

The presence of my children in my life fills me with emotional and physical vitality. I feel revived when they are with me. Whenever I watch the smiles on their faces, it feels as if my sufferings are nothing compared to this reward. Through God, anything is possible. I believe that He will protect us all, till the end.

Miraculously, my children, my siblings, their children, and other family and relatives have begun to communicate with me again. Thanks be to God! Our family, after almost forty years, wants to have a family reunion. Even through the quarantine of the COVID-19 virus, and now war between

Russia and Ukraine, our finances continue to support us, and life in general is much improved. Amazingly, my business is doing exceedingly well, so I am able to pay a management company to take over for me. Everything has started to turn around.

I am catching up and am doing much better than I was forty years ago. We are blessed and enjoy our house on the big lake and now also own a vacation home only a mile from the beach. God was, is, and will be with us throughout our journey in the years to come.

While many unheard voices continue to cry for justice, my heart shouts many thanks to our Divine Holy Spirit for His deliverance, protection, and reconciliation.

Our Lord's faithful followers conquered communism. Through His grace, we have overcome. Through His grace, we live in true accomplishment and victory.

Thanks be to God!

EPILOGUE

I like to perceive *power* as a metaphor for the strength that has enabled me to survive the ebb and flow that life offers. This word explains the survival instincts that come out when the world goes against a person.

I didn't have that inclination in me, or maybe it surfaced at the right time. But I didn't identify myself as a strong person initially. However, the events I have lived through are evidence of my inner strength. You wouldn't imagine that anyone weak could live through such brutality and injustice. I built this inclination, this propensity. I honed my power. I became an active individual who takes life by the reins and leads it in a meaningful way. The power in me surfaced—not because I summoned it or desired it, but because God knew I needed it.

His power has enabled me to survive the ebb life has offered.

Appendix A

PHOTOGRAPHS

My father, Tribunal Justice Judge, Senator Kuy Peou

Angkor Wat, Cambodia

Harvesting rubber sap

My father, a senator

My brother, Visothara (Scott)
He trained as a pilot in Thailand then worked
for Khmer Akas airline.

Appendix B

COMFORTING VERSES

To help readers understand my true experience, this is an overview of many of the horrors that happened to millions of Asian families like mine, and yet it also details—in the order I later remembered them—a summary of my own convoluted tales to shed light on our family's incredible survival in the era historians have described as "the killing fields." For comfort, I think of how my experiences relate to holy verses.

> *The Light shines in the darkness, and the darkness did not comprehend it. . . . The world did not know Him.*
>
> —John 1:5, 10 NASB 1995

During the hardest days, I was taken to be killed by Khmer Rouge soldiers three different times, but God performed unbelievable miracles to spare my life. At that time, I didn't know God existed. Now I love these words about Him:

You are the God who performs miracles;
you display your power among the peoples.

—Psalm 77:14

I, along with some family members, lived for years in a concentration camp, where everyone was forced to do hard labor. The guards starved us. We became sick; all communication was cut off from the whole world, and we were not allowed to walk anywhere without permission from the group leader. After the war was over, our lives were no longer the same, and we were no longer the same. We had lost our parents, our older and younger brothers, other relatives, and the properties our parents owned. Soon, our siblings were scattered all over the world. Today some of them live in France and Australia, and I live in the United States.

But your iniquities have separated
you from your God.

—Isaiah 59:2

Living in the US with two small children, I worked for the federal government for several years in Boston, and the three of us did well and lived harmoniously together. Up to this point, I did not appreciate what God had given to me, and my sins separated me from God and blinded me and caused me to suffer and not function well during cold weather.

Although you have been forsaken and hated,
with no one traveling through.

—Isaiah 60:15

Without thinking clearly, I decided to move south to Florida to find a warmer place to live, and eventually we ended up in South Carolina. Not long after we moved away from the big city I was lost in a new world without any family, job, friends, and relatives. It was just me and two small children.

Among which I scatter you, . . .
I will not let you go entirely unpunished.

—Jeremiah 30:11

When we moved to Columbia, South Carolina, I bought a house next to Ted. A few years later Ted and I were married, but our marriage turned into anything but a fairy tale. For the first five years of our marriage, his mother turned our lives upside down with mental abuse that I did my best to hide from my children. My irritation and emotions broke through, however. They didn't understand what was going on, they ended up running away from home.

All your allies have forgotten you;
they care nothing for you.

—Jeremiah 30:14

I faced many facets of trials, pains, suffering, tribulations, grief, and loneliness. I lost the ability to keep my young children by my side, and I was not able to provide for them. Ever since then, our relationship became distant. They have a right to hate me, because I lost the ability to comfort them when they were growing up and really needed me.

For the LORD *disciplines those he loves.*

—Hebrews 12:6 NLT

My husband had a feeble personality and was later diagnosed with Parkinson's disease. A few years later my brother David moved back to live with us. Nevertheless, the absence of my children and the power of love for them pushed me to do something that would help them. I decided to start a real estate business even though I had no experience. I had to deal with crooks, contractors, and bad tenants, which pushed us further into a financial dilemma. I was falling into a dark bottomless pit. I couldn't count on my husband to help because he got nervous so easily and couldn't deal with obstacles. Both children were gone by themselves, with no one to shelter them, and we all struggled on our own. With no one to turn to, I cried out to God for help. Without hope I surrendered myself completely to Him, repenting of my sin, and He is the ultimate answer to everything.

"I will give you back your health
and heal your wounds," says the LORD.

—Jeremiah 30:17

Twenty years later, in my land of suffering, God granted me sixteen rental properties, all paid off. Our lives continue to be victorious. Each of our businesses is doing well, and I am proud of how much both children have accomplished on their own. My grandson and both of my children live blessed and successful lives.

As you read this book, through a journey lasting over sixty years and spanning halfway across the world, you will learn of God's delivering power. You will read of my experiences with city life in Cambodia when I was young, in the communist Khmer Rouge killing fields, and then in the United States.

I have lived in Phnom Penh, Massachusetts, Florida, and South Carolina. I have experienced too many deaths, much deep sorrow, isolation, and rejection. But along with the suffering has also come great joy, family togetherness, love, and victory. What may surprise you is that the killing fields may not have been the worst part of my life, nor the easiest to survive.

In the end, there is victory with God's help. Without His protection, again and again, you would not be reading about my victories. God is the only one who knows what is inside my heart and my soul. He purposely saved my life several times. There must have been a reason. My heart means good, but my actions left me vulnerable. Life without the support of someone strong to help one another is as bad as a house without a foundation or without a roof.

Appendix C

POLITICAL BACKGROUND EVENTS

October 19, 1966 CIA intel from radio broadcast from Phnom Penh in French to Southeast Asia

The US political and military intervention in countries of our region is the main cause of the present crisis. Prince Chief of State Norodom Sihanouk stated in an interview granted to Socolo d'itala, organ of the Italian Social Movement. Cessation of US interventions would be necessary to put an end to this crisis which is threatening the world, the prince added. The Asian people, like the western peoples, have the right to solve their internal affairs as they like. Therefore it is stupid to think they can agree to renounce their independence in order to abide by political and colonialism, under whatever form, can no longer be imposed on Asia. Although tension still exists among many Asian countries, I have the conviction that it will be settled among Asians. US intervention in these affairs can only make its solution more difficult. Prince Norodom Sihanouk then blamed the US for having always refused to recognize Cambodial neutrality as a definitive fact, for having plotted against the Cambodian regime, for having refused to recognize the present Cambodian borders and for having stepping up the attacks on and destruction of the Khmer border villages. The prince added that it is obvious the US government will be satisfied only when it succeeds in imposing on Cambodia a regime similar to that of Bangkok or Saigon. . . . after stressing ties of friendship with the Chinese People's Republic, Prince Sihanouk spoke of Buddhism and the Pope's action. The US aggression in Vietnam and the genocide committed by the US forces against the Vietnamese seem to be the product of a country that refers to Christian civilization. Buddhists, such as we are, wish that the Holy Father would proceed to southeast Asia to denounce, as General DeGaulle has just done, the criminal war waged by the US aggressors against a people who ask for nothing but peace. So, it is certain that a statement by the Pope would condemn the US aggression, save tens of millions of human beings, and help therefore avoid a possible world war. With regard to communism, Prince Norodom Sihanouk affirmed that each country in southeast Asia has the right to adopt whatever regime it thinks can help it solve its problems. Such is the case of the Cambodian people who, linked to the throne and Buddhism, have achieved a perfect national unity amid a people's socialist community.*

* Central Intelligence Agency, *Daily Report, Foreign Radio Broadcasts, Issues 201–205, 1966* (Columbus, OH: Ohio State University, digitized November 7, 2017).

October 20, 1966 Radio transmission regarding South Vietnam/US from LIBERATION PRESS AGENCY

The US schemes . . . aggressors had expanded their war in both North and South Vietnam, conducted daily raids against the SV people and increasing bombing raids on NV. They are planning to double the number of US expeditionary troops in SV and are calling for the sending of more mercenaries there. Meanwhile, to cover up their new peace proposals, the statement added. In such a conjuncture and judging from the composition of the Manila conference, it is clear that this conference aims at nothing but increasing the collusion between the US and its henchmen and pushing further war against the people in Vietnam and Asia as a whole. This conference is also an opportunity for the US imperialists to bring to the political stage their henchmen and satellites who will be asked to join in prattling about peace so as to extricate the Johnson clique from their stalemate, help them win more votes at the November elections, and deceive the American public opinion. . . . The SVietnamese people are highly indignant at this vile political maneuver of the US imperialists and their flunkeys, and regard it as a challenge to the people in SV and Asia and the peace-loving people all over the world.*

* Central Intelligence Agency, *Daily Report, Foreign Radio Broadcasts, Issues 201–205,* 1966 (Columbus, OH: Ohio State University, digitized November 7, 2017).

Appendix D

CHRONOLOGY OF CAMBODIAN EVENTS

Cambodia's political darkness lasted for fifteen years. From 1970 to 1985, Cambodia had five political leaders:

1970—King Norodom Sihanouk left.
1970–1975—Lon Nol took over.
1975–1979—The Khmer Rouge conquered and ruled.
1979–1989—The Vietnamese invaded and occupied Cambodia.
1985–present—Hun Sen serves as prime minister.

However, the seeds of Cambodia's political unrest were sown much earlier.

1863 Cambodia becomes a protectorate of France.*

1941 Prince Norodom Sihanouk becomes king. Japan occupies Cambodia during World War II.

1945 Japanese occupation ends. France reimposes its protectorate.

1946 General elections are held for the first time. Communist guerrillas rise against the French.

1950 Cambodian communists join forces with Vietnamese against French colonialism.†

1953 Cambodia gains independence from France. King Sihanouk renames it the Kingdom of Cambodia.

1954 Geneva Conference: French withdraw from Cambodia, Vietnam, and Laos.†

1954–70 The Kingdom of Cambodia is an autocratic monarchy, nonaligned in foreign policy, and neutral in the Vietnam War.†

* Entries marked by an asterisk are from "Cambodia Profile—Timeline," BBC News, July 20, 2018, https://www.bbc.com/news/world-asia-pacific-13006828.

† Entries marked by a dagger are from Ben Kiernan, "Chronology of Cambodian Events, 1950–1999," Yale University, Genocide Studies Program, https://gsp.yale.edu/case-studies/cambodian-genocide-program/publications/chronology-cambodian-events-1950. Used by permission, Ben Kiernan, Director, Cambodian Genocide Program, Yale University.

1955 Sihanouk abdicates to become prime minister. His father, Norodom Suramarit, becomes king.

1960 King Norodom Suramarit dies. Sihanouk becomes head of state.*

1962 Cambodian Communist leader Tou Samouth disappears. Pol Pot replaces him and makes plans for a rebellion. Visits China and Vietnam, 1964–65.†

1965 Sihanouk allows North Vietnamese guerrillas to set up bases in Cambodia in order to fight the US in the Vietnam War.

1965 US escalation of Vietnam War; Vietnamese communist forces increasingly seek sanctuary in Cambodia. Sihanouk breaks relations with US while continuing to crack down on domestic communists and other dissenters.†

1967 Pol Pot group of Cambodian communists ("Khmer Rouge") launch an insurgency against Sihanouk in northwest Cambodia. Brutal government repression.†

1969 US B-52 bombardment of Vietnamese sanctuaries in Cambodia begins.†

1970–75 The Khmer Republic. Coup against Sihanouk establishes General Lon Nol as president of a US-backed regime, the Khmer Republic. Sihanouk, in exile in China, joins forces with the Vietnamese and the Khmer Rouge. Lon Nol's rule initially wins the support of the urban classes but becomes increasingly dictatorial.†

1973 US B-52 bombardment of Cambodian countryside in support of Lon Nol forces reaches its peak. 250,000 tons of bombs are dropped in seven months before US Congress calls a halt to the bombing on August 15. Toll from 1969 to 1973: 50,000 to 150,000 civilian deaths from the bombing. Pol Pot forces use the bombing's killing and destruction as recruitment propaganda and as an excuse for the abandonment of moderate socialist policies in the insurgent zones. Purges of moderate communists suspected of disloyalty to Pol Pot.[†]

1975 Khmer Rouge forces led by Pol Pot defeat Lon Nol army and take Phnom Penh on April 17, 1975. Cities immediately evacuated, and the country is cut off from the outside world. Killings of surrendered Lon Nol officers, soldiers, and officials. Forced unpaid agricultural labor for all, and brutal persecution of Buddhist monks and ethnic minorities: Chinese, Vietnamese, Cham Muslim, and Thai.[†] The educated middle class are tortured and executed. Some die from starvation or disease. The death toll over the next three years is estimated at 1.7 million.

1975–79 Democratic Kampuchea (DK)[†]

1976 Massive starvation in parts of northwest Cambodia, following the deportation there of hundreds of thousands of evacuated urban dwellers. DK government announced with Khieu Samphan as Head of State, Pol Pot as Prime Minister, Ieng Sary and Son

Sen as Deputy Prime Ministers. Zone commanders Chhit Choeun (alias Mok) and Ke Pauk assume control of the DK army. Pol Pot remains Secretary-General of the secretive Communist Party of Kampuchea, and Nuon Chea is Deputy Secretary.[†]

1977 A second wave of bloody purges convulses Cambodia, centrally directed by Pol Pot group, which attempts to eliminate all dissident communists and other moderates and recalcitrants. The purges spread to the mass of the peasantry as well as to the persecuted urban evacuees. Cambodia also launches military attacks across all three of its borders, massacring civilians in Thailand, Vietnam, and Laos.[†]

1978 Cambodia declines to negotiate with Vietnam over the border war. Domestically, massive purges spark an uprising in eastern zone of Cambodia in opposition to the Pol Pot regime. Rebels are defeated and regroup across the Vietnamese border and call for help from Hanoi.[†]

1979–89 Vietnamese troops invade and overthrow Pol Pot regime. People's Republic of Kampuchea is established.[†] Life begins to return to its previous standard before the Khmer Rouge takeover. Former eastern zone rebel Heng Samrin is proclaimed president, Hun Sen foreign minister (later prime minister).[†]

1981 The pro-Vietnamese Kampuchean People's Revolutionary Party wins parliamentary elections. The rest of Asia and the West refuse to recognize the new government. The DK, a government-in-exile, which includes the Khmer Rouge and Sihanouk, retains its seat at the United Nations because it sees Vietnam's actions as a violation of the UN charter.

1985 Hun Sen becomes prime minister. Guerrilla warfare forces hundreds of thousands to become refugees.

1989 First Paris Conference on Cambodia fails. Vietnamese troops withdraw from Cambodia. Pol Pot's Khmer Rouge and their allies (including Sihanouk) resume their attempt to retake power from Hun Sen's newly proclaimed State of Cambodia (SOC).†

1990 Formation of the Supreme National Council (SNC), composed of six SOC members and two from each of the three opposition factions, including former DK President Khieu Samphan and Deputy Prime Minister Son Sen.†

1991 Paris Agreement on Cambodia signed on October 23 by the four Cambodian factions and eighteen foreign ministers of interested countries. Khmer Rouge forces signed the agreement but declined to abide by its provisions for ceasefire, UN supervision, demobilization, and disarmament.†

1993 General elections, boycotted by Khmer Rouge, which continues its attacks on government forces. Coalition government formed by Prince Norodom Ranariddh's FUNCINPEC party, which won a plurality, and Hun Sen's Cambodian People's Party

(CPP).† Sihanouk is reinstalled as king. The country is renamed the Kingdom of Cambodia. The DK loses its seat at the UN.

1994 Khmer Rouge movement outlawed by Cambodia's National Assembly.†

1996 Khmer Rouge forces split, with Ieng Sary defecting to the government in return for an amnesty.†

1997 Turmoil within Khmer Rouge. Pol Pot executes Son Sen and is in turn placed under house arrest by Mok, Nuon Chea, and Khieu Samphan.† The Khmer Rouge sentence Pol Pot to life in prison. Hun Sen overthrows Prince Ranariddh and replaces him with Ung Huot. The coup attracts international condemnation.

1998 Mutiny against Mok by Khmer Rouge units led by Ke Pauk, who joins forces with the government side. Pol Pot dies. General elections return People's Party/FUNCINPEC coalition to power, dominated by Hun Sen. Nuon Chea and Khieu Samphan surrender to Hun Sen. Mok remains the last Khmer Rouge leader still at large.†

1999 A United Nations Commission of Experts recommends the creation of an international tribunal and truth commission to judge the crimes of the Khmer Rouge period. Mok is captured by Cambodian army and sent before a military tribunal. Former DK prison commandant Kang Khek Ieu (alias Duch) is also arrested.†

2002 First multiparty local elections are held; the ruling Cambodian People's Party wins 98 percent of the communes.

2003 Hun Sen's Cambodian People's Party wins the general elections but does not win enough of a majority to govern alone.

2004 King Sihanouk abdicates and is succeeded by his son Norodom Sihamoni.*

2005 Tribunal to try Khmer Rouge leaders receives approval from UN.

2007 Most senior surviving Khmer Rouge member, Nuon Chea "Brother Number Two," is arrested and charged with crimes against humanity.*

2009 Former Khmer Rouge leader Kaing Guek Eav, known as Duch and head of the Tuol Sleng prison camp, goes on trial for crimes against humanity.

2010 Kaing Guek Eav is found guilty and sentenced to 35 years.†

2015 Prime Minister Hun Sen marks 30 years in power.

ABOUT THE AUTHOR

Vera Peou Crenshaw is a survivor of the Khmer Rouge killing fields of Cambodia.

The story of her near-death experiences during the communist killing fields and numerous trials afterward, through miracles and with God's help, will take you with her through the jungles of Cambodia, the streets of Boston, down to Florida, and on to South Carolina where she and her children would face some of their greatest challenges on the path to their greatest triumphs and victories.